Glutenless

Maximus

Over 300 gluten free favorites
for those who don't like
"gluten freaky" food

Printed in USA
ISBN-13: 978-1505384765

For Kaia, Ross and Isaac

(The ones who coined the term "gluten freaky"
for bad tasting gluten free food.)

Happy Cooking!

Enjoy!
Heidi Likins

Welcome To Glutenless Maximus!
A gluten free cook book

All recipes in this cookbook use the same gluten free flour mix whenever it says "flour."

A not so "gluten freaky" flour mix

A good gluten free flour mix is essential to creating appetizing gluten free food. Some gluten free recipes in circulation use various flour combinations that may work better for that particular recipe. But the recipes in this book sacrifice the little extra that you gain from different flours for the convenience of one mix for everything. So far the little extra hasn't been missed.

The mix that follows is the one used throughout this book. It balances a silky starch with the texture of rice flour to best imitate wheat flour. Some gluten free flour mixes sold in stores are very similar and may also work well.

Basic Flour Mix:

1 cup brown rice flour
2 cups corn starch *or* tapioca flour
~~1 tablespoon potato flour (not potato starch)~~

Easy Big Batch:

4 cups brown rice flour
2 boxes of corn starch *or* 4 cups tapioca flour
~~¼ cup potato flour (not potato starch)~~

The potato flour can be left out if you're sensitive to nightshades,
or can't find it easily. But the mix works better with it included.

If you want to do lots of baking, mix up a big batch before you get started!

Converting Recipes to Gluten Free

We all have our favorite recipes and most can fairly easily be converted to gluten free. So pull out your most loved recipes and simply convert them!

First of all, it's helpful to know what gluten is and what it does.

Gluten is a protein in wheat, barley, and rye that holds everything together. This is important for baked goods as they tend to crumble, but not as important with main dishes. To make up for the lack of gluten, there needs to be more protein in the recipe along with something like xanthan gum or guar gum to hold your baked items together.

Gluten is also a preservative. That means gluten free baked goods go stale faster that wheat items. So, only make what can be eaten in a day or two, or freeze what's left over. Most gluten free baked goods freeze well.

General principles for converting main dishes:

- Not much change is usually necessary.
- Make sure you are using all gluten free ingredients, especially check spices and seasonings.
- Substitute corn starch or gluten free flour as a thickener for gravies and sauces.
- Avoid any recipe that calls for ingredients that don't have gluten free alternatives.

General principles for converting baked goods:

These can take little more work, but they're certainly not impossible.

The first main issue is getting things to rise well. Gluten free baked goods tend to be heavy. The second, is getting them to stick together and not crumble.

- Add more egg – usually 1 extra egg does the trick. This helps increase the protein content and helps the ingredients bond. It also helps with leavening (rising). You may need to adjust the amount of liquid in the recipe if you add an extra egg - see the next step. If the recipe already calls for four or more eggs, you don't need to add any extra.

- Flour, fat (oil/butter) and liquid (milk/water) amounts usually stay the same. Cut back on the liquid amount by ¼ cup for every extra egg you add.

- Add some xanthan gum. This replaces the binding power of gluten. Usually around ¼-⅓ teaspoon per cup of flour works well.

- Baking powder/soda amounts usually stay the same.

- If you find your gluten free version is too heavy, try adding some egg replacer. This is also a leavening agent. ¼ -½ teaspoon per cup of flour usually helps baked goods rise better. Or increase the baking powder or baking soda just a little. Too much leavening will cause things to bubble over and make a mess in your oven, so be careful.

- The batter may be runnier than wheat cake or muffin recipes. Some brands of xanthan gum make a thicker batter than others, but all have good finished results in the baked item.

  The only exception to this is if you're making something that has fruit suspended in the center of the baked item, such as blueberry muffins. With a thinner batter, they will sink to the bottom. Sometimes just letting the batter sit for a few minutes allows it to thicken up.

- Give it a try. If your recipe doesn't come out right, tweak ingredients and amounts the next time you try it.

- Low altitude cooks can try substituting citrus flavored carbonated beverages for the milk or other liquid. This can help baked goods rise.

- Beating the egg whites separately can also help lighten cakes and muffins.

- Bake according to the original recipe.

- Flops will happen, but don't give up! When you get it right, the home made items are well worth the effort!

One Example:

Honey Muffins

(From *Taste of Home* magazine, April/May 2007)

Original Version:

2 cups all-purpose wheat flour
½ cup sugar
1½ teaspoons baking powder
½ teaspoon salt
1 egg
1 cup milk
¼ cup butter, melted
¼ cup honey

Gluten Free Version:

2 cups gluten free flour
½ cup sugar
1½ teaspoons baking powder
½ teaspoon salt
2 eggs
¾ cup milk
¼ cup butter, melted
¼ cup honey
½ teaspoon xanthan gum

Follow the recipe directions given in the original version. A slightly reduced version of this recipe is in the muffins section (see page 58).

Breads:

Gluten free breads are completely different creatures than wheat breads. They are batter breads that don't have to be kneaded. Kneading is used to bring out the stickiness of the gluten in the wheat flour. Something you don't have to worry about. Regular yeast bread recipes turn out dense and dry, and there's really no use trying to directly convert these recipes. If there's a bread recipe that you really love, with some interesting ingredients, use a tried and true gluten free bread recipe. Then add the extra ingredients that make it unique - as long as they are gluten free ingredients.

Altitude adjustments for low altitude cooks:

All the recipes in this book have been developed at high altitude. (Around 7000 feet above sea level.) That means the sugar and baking powder may have been reduced slightly, liquid increased, and the oven temperature increased slightly.

If you find the baked items in this book aren't coming out as beautifully as you would like, try a few of these adjustments:

- **Increase the baking powder:** for each teaspoon, increase by ¼ teaspoon.
- **Increase sugar:** for each cup, increase by 1 to 3 tablespoons.
- **Decrease liquid:** for each cup, reduce by 2 to 3 tablespoons.
- **Decrease oven temperature** by 25 degrees F.

Gluten Free Pantry Staples

Must Haves:

These can be found at most grocery stores or at health food stores.

Xanthan Gum: A powder that replaces the stickiness of gluten. You can't bake gluten free without it or something similar, like guar gum. It can be found in most grocery and health food stores. It's a bit expensive, but a little goes a long way. One bag should last months.

Egg Replacer: This is a leavening agent. It helps keep gluten free baked goods from coming out too heavy.

Rice Flour, Potato Flour, and Tapioca Flour or Corn Starch: for your flour mix

Other Good Ingredients:

Flax seed meal: This can be added to breads, etc. when you are wanting to replace that whole wheat taste and texture.

Almond Flour and/or Rice Bran: These add texture and taste that helps mimic wheat.

Gluten Free Oats: Oats have a gluten protein, but it's slightly different from the one in wheat, barley and rye. Some people will still react to it even if it's certified gluten free. The problem with regular oats is that they are processed on the same equipment as wheat, so are contaminated. Look for the oats that say they are gluten free.

A Few Important Notes

- GF means gluten free. Make sure all the ingredients you use are gluten free.

- Xanthan gums vary. Some make a thin batter and other make thicker batter. If your baked item has very thin batter, let it sit for a few minutes to see if it will thicken before adding a little more flour.

- All flours have slightly different moisture levels. You may need to tweak the recipes just a little to accommodate these variations.

- Any recipe with an * after it is one that can be made in about 30 minutes.

- The recipes within each section are alphabetized.

- Carbohydrate counts are approximated and not intended to be exact calculations. When only a total carb count is given, divide by the number of servings to get the carb count per-serving.

- Cookbooks are always a work in progress. There's lots of white space in this book that you can fill with your notes on what works, what doesn't, and ways you've improved the recipe. Make it your own!

leave out egg replacer

Table of Contents

Yeast Breads

Basic White Bread

(Or real bread as the kids call it)

1 tablespoon yeast
1 tablespoon sugar
¼ cup very warm water

1¾ cups flour
4 tablespoons sugar
2 teaspoons xanthan gum
2 teaspoons egg replacer
2 teaspoons baking powder
1½ teaspoons salt
1 teaspoon vinegar
¼ cup butter, melted
¾ cup warm milk
1 egg plus 4 egg whites *or* 1 egg and ⅓ cup egg white substitute *or* 3 eggs

Heat the oven to 350° and grease a standard loaf pan. Mix the yeast, 1 tablespoon sugar, and very warm water in a small bowl. Set aside and allow to rise. In a large mixing bowl, combine the remaining ingredients and add the yeast mixture. Beat with an electric mixer or whisk until well incorporated and the batter thickens. Pour the batter into the loaf pan and bake for 30 minutes. Cover the loaf with foil and bake for 30 minutes longer or until dark golden brown. The bread will fall slightly as it cools.

Total carbs 240g
About 17g carbs per ¹⁄₁₄ slice

Basic White Bread Variations

❖ *Buns:*
Spoon the batter into the cups of a greased whoopie pie pan and bake for 20 minutes.

❖ *Bread Sticks:*
Using a pastry bag with only the inner plastic coupling, pipe the batter into straight lines on a greased cookie sheet and bake for 20 minutes.

❖ *Hotdog Buns:*
Using a pastry bag with only the inner plastic coupling, pipe the batter onto a greased cookie sheet in pairs of straight lines that touch each other. Each line will become one side of the hot dog bun. Bake 20 minutes.

❖ *Soft Pretzels:*
Using a pastry bag with only the inner plastic coupling, pipe into pretzel shapes on a greased cookie sheet and sprinkle with coarse salt. Bake 20 minutes.

❖ *Mongolian Borzig (Fried Bread):*
Mix in 1 more cup of flour and roll the dough out on a well-floured surface until it's ½ inch thick. Cut into diamonds about 1 inch by 2 inches and allow to rise in a warm place. Deep fry the bread in 2 inches of oil hot enough to make a drop of water sizzle. Cook until golden on both sides, flipping at least once. Drain on paper towels and serve warm.

Brown Bread

1 tablespoon yeast
1 tablespoon sugar
¼ cup very warm water

1½ cups flour
¼ cup rice bran
¼ cup flax seed meal
½ cup GF oats
¼ cup sugar
2 teaspoons xanthan gum

2 teaspoons egg replacer
2 teaspoons baking powder
1½ teaspoons salt

1 teaspoon vinegar
¼ cup butter, melted
¾ cup warm milk
4 tablespoons molasses
3 eggs

Preheat the oven to 350°. Grease a loaf pan well. Mix the yeast, 1 tablespoon sugar, and very warm water in a small bowl and allow to rise. Mix the dry ingredients in a large bowl. Add the wet ingredients, vinegar through eggs, along with the yeast mixture.

Using a stiff whisk, mix well. The dough will look more like a very thick batter. Place the dough in the prepared pan. Bake for 1 hour or until golden brown. Makes one loaf.

Total carbs 240g
About 17g carbs per 14th slice

Cinnamon Gorilla Bread

Pan:
2 tablespoons butter, melted
¼ cup brown sugar

1 batch of Basic White Bread (see page 14)

Filling:
3 tablespoons brown sugar
¼ cup cinnamon sugar

2 tablespoons raisins
2 tablespoons walnuts

Glaze:
1½ tablespoons butter, softened
½ cup powdered sugar
¼ teaspoon vanilla
1 tablespoon milk

Preheat the oven to 350°. Spread the melted butter and brown sugar in a 9x9 pan or bundt pan. Make a batch of Basic White Bread dough and place it in a pastry bag fitted only with the inner plastic coupling, or a zipper bag with one corner cut off. Put a thin layer of dough dots on the bottom of the pan. Mix the brown sugar and cinnamon sugar in a small bowl. Sprinkle the dough in the pan with half of the brown sugar mixture, as well as half the raisins and walnuts.

Add another lay of dough dots on top and sprinkle with the remaining sugar mixture, raisins and walnuts. Cover with more dough dots until the dough is used up. Bake for 20 - 25 minutes.

Mix the glaze ingredients together in a small bowl while the bread is baking. Invert the bread immediately onto a plate as soon as it comes out of the oven. Serve warm with glaze drizzled over the top.

Total carbs 445g

Cinnamon Rolls

1 batch of Basic White Bread (see page 14)
1 cup flour

3 tablespoons butter, melted
¼ cup brown sugar

⅓ cup butter, melted
⅔ cup brown sugar
1 tablespoon cinnamon

Chopped pecans or walnuts (optional)
Raisins (optional)

Preheat the oven to 350° and spread the 3 tablespoons melted butter and ¼ cup brown sugar in a 9x13 pan.

Add the extra cup of flour to the Basic White Bread dough. Dump the dough out on a very well-floured piece of plastic wrap. Sprinkle the dough with a generous amount of flour. Using another piece of plastic wrap on top, or well-floured fingers, press the dough into a rectangular shape.

Remove the top piece of plastic wrap. In a small bowl, mix the butter, brown sugar, and cinnamon. Sprinkle the dough with the cinnamon sugar mixture and any other desired toppings. Using the bottom layer of plastic wrap, roll up the dough starting on the long side. Cut into 1 inch slices and very carefully place each roll in the pan lined with butter and brown sugar. They will be very soft. Bake 15-20 minutes. Immediately invert onto a plate and serve. Drizzle with the glaze from the Cinnamon Gorilla Bread if desired.

Total carbs 423g
Plus any carbs from optional toppings used (30g carbs for ¼ cup raisins)

Coconut Pudding Rolls

Dry ingredients:
2 cups flour
3 tablespoons sugar
1 teaspoon xanthan gum
¾ teaspoon egg replacer
½ teaspoon baking powder
½ teaspoon salt
2¼ teaspoons yeast

Wet ingredients:
1 egg
3 tablespoons butter, melted
½ teaspoon vinegar
½ cup warm milk

Topping:
3 tablespoons sugar
2 tablespoons flour
1 cup coconut milk

Preheat the oven to warm and grease a 9x9 pan. Mix the dry ingredients in a large bowl. Add the wet ingredients to the center of the flour mixture and mix until it forms a very stiff batter. Using well-floured or wet hands, form the batter into balls, about 2 inches in diameter. Place the balls in the pan and allow to rise in the warm oven for about 30 minutes.

Remove the rolls and increase the oven to 350°. Mix the topping ingredients and pour over the rolls. Bake for about 25-30 minutes or until the rolls are done. Serve warm.

Total carbs 306g
About 34g carbs per roll

Flat Bread

2 cups flour
1 teaspoon xanthan gum
1 teaspoon sugar
1 teaspoon salt
1 teaspoon yeast
1 tablespoon oil
1 cup warm milk

Preheat the oven to warm and grease several cookie sheets. In a large bowl, mix all ingredients. Form the dough into balls about the size of your fist and roll out ¼ inch thick between two sheets of well-floured plastic wrap. Remove the top layer of plastic and flip the dough onto the cookie sheets, then remove the bottom layer of plastic wrap. Allow to rise in the warm oven for 30 minutes. Cook the bread in batches in a dry skillet over medium-high heat for about 3 minutes on each side or until done and lightly browned.

Total carbs 218g

Flour Tortillas

2 cups flour
1 teaspoon xanthan gum
1 teaspoon sugar
1 teaspoon salt
1 tablespoon oil
1 cup milk

In a large bowl, mix all ingredients into a very stiff dough. Using egg sized pieces of dough, roll out tortillas on a well-floured surface. Cook in a dry frying pan over medium-high heat until lightly browned on each side. Keep warm until ready to serve. Makes about 6 tortillas.

Total carbs 218g
About 36g carbs per tortilla

Focaccia Bread

Dry ingredients:
2¼ cups flour
2 teaspoons xanthan gum
1 teaspoon egg replacer
1 teaspoon salt
2 tablespoons sugar
2¼ teaspoons yeast
¾ teaspoon garlic powder
¾ teaspoon oregano
¾ teaspoon thyme
¾ teaspoon basil
¼ teaspoon black pepper

Wet ingredients:
1 egg, plus 1 egg white
3 tablespoons olive oil
½ teaspoon vinegar
1 tablespoon honey
⅔ cup warm milk

Topping:
2 tablespoons olive oil
2 tablespoons parmesan cheese
¼ teaspoon garlic salt

Preheat the oven to warm for rising. Grease a 9 inch round cake pan. Mix the dry ingredients in a large bowl. Add the wet ingredients and mix together. Place the dough in the prepared pan. Smooth the top with a wet spatula. Make small indentations over the top of the dough with your fingertips. Pour olive oil over the top and sprinkle on the parmesan cheese and garlic salt. Allow to rise in the warm oven for 30 minutes. Remove the bread. Increase the oven to 350°. Bake for 30 minutes, or until golden brown.

Total carbs 262g

Grandma's Oatmeal Bread

1¼ cups milk
½ cup GF oats

1 tablespoon yeast
1 tablespoon sugar
¼ cup very warm water

2 cups flour
2 tablespoons sugar
2 teaspoons xanthan gum

2 teaspoons egg replacer
2 teaspoons baking powder
1½ teaspoons salt

3 eggs
1 teaspoon vinegar
¼ cup butter, melted
4 tablespoons molasses

Preheat the oven to 350°. Grease a loaf pan well. Mix the milk and oats in a small bowl and cook in the microwave for about 2 minutes. In another small bowl, mix the yeast, sugar, and warm water and set aside to rise. Meanwhile, mix the dry ingredients in a large bowl, flour through salt.

Add the egg, vinegar, melted butter, and molasses to the center of the dry ingredients and then pour the oatmeal mixture on top along with the yeast mixture. Using a stiff whisk, mix the dough, starting in the center and gradually adding in the outer flour. Place the dough in the prepared loaf pan. Bake for 1 hour or until golden brown.

Total carbs 240g
About 17g carbs per 14th slice

Orange Ring

Dough:
1 batch of Basic White Bread (see page 14)
1 cup flour

Filling:
⅓ cup butter, almost melted
¼ cup sugar
2 tablespoons orange zest

Glaze:
1½ cups powdered sugar
2 teaspoons butter
½ teaspoon vanilla
2-3 tablespoons orange juice
2 teaspoons orange zest

Preheat the oven to warm and grease a cookie sheet. Make the Basic White Bread recipe, adding the extra cup of flour to the dough. On a well-floured, plastic wrap covered surface, use well-floured hands to spread the dough into a large rectangle. Spread the butter on the dough and sprinkle on the sugar and orange zest. Using the plastic wrap, and starting on the long side, roll the dough into a log. Join the two ends of the log to make a ring.

Transfer the ring to the cookie sheet. Using a scissors, snip the dough every 1½ inches around the outside, being careful not to snip all the way through the log. Twist each section so that the inside swirl is facing up. Allow to rise for 30 minutes in the warm oven.

Remove the ring and increase the oven to 350°. Bake for 20-25 minutes. Mix all the glaze ingredients in a small bowl. When the ring is cool, drizzle with the glaze. Makes about 12 rolls.

Total carbs 430g
About 36g carbs per roll

Pita Bread

3 cups flour
2 teaspoons xanthan gum
1 teaspoon salt
4 teaspoons yeast
3 tablespoons sugar
3 tablespoons oil
2½ cups warm milk

Place the 3 cups of flour, xanthan gum, and salt in a stand mixer bowl with the paddle attachment. Add the yeast, sugar, and oil, mixing well. Slowly pour the milk in and mix until well blended.

Place the dough in an oiled bowl, cover with plastic wrap and allow to rise in a warm place for 1 hour or until nearly double in size.

Preheat the oven to 475°. Divide the dough into 8-10 pieces. Using your hands, roll each piece into a ball and place on a well-floured surface. Using your fingertips, spread the dough out into a disc about ¼ inch thick. Avoid pressing down on the edges.

Dust excess flour off each round. Place 2 to 3 rounds on a pizza crisper – a pizza pan with holes in it. Don't let edges touch. Bake for 5-8 minutes, until lightly browned on the outside. Remove from oven and cut in half. If the pita didn't puff up, use a knife and very gently cut the pitas open. Repeat until all the dough is cooked.

Total carbs 425g

Thick Pizza Crust

1 tablespoon yeast
1 tablespoon sugar
½ cup warm water

2 tablespoons butter
⅓ cup milk
2 cups flour
1½ tablespoons sugar

1 teaspoon xanthan gum
1 teaspoon egg replacer
1 teaspoon baking powder
½ teaspoon salt
1 teaspoon vinegar
1 egg, plus 1 egg white

2 tablespoons olive oil

Preheat the oven to 350°. In a small bowl mix the yeast, sugar, and warm water. Set aside to rise. In a small bowl, melt the butter in the microwave and then add the milk to the butter and heat one more minute, or until it's very warm.

In a large bowl mix all the remaining ingredients through the egg white, including the milk mixture and the yeast mixture. You should have a dough you can roll out. Place the dough on a greased pizza pan. Roll until very thin, about ¼ inch. You'll probably need to use your fingers to spread the dough to the edges of the pan. Bake for 10 minutes.

Remove the crust from the pan and place it on the counter. Spread the remaining olive oil on the empty pan and put the pan back in the oven. Don't leave in the oven for more than 5 minutes or the oil will burn. Top the pizza crust with any desired toppings. Remove the pan from the oven. Be careful, it will be very hot! Place the pizza back on the pan and bake for 20-25 minutes or until the cheese is melted.

Total carbs 270g
About 33g carbs per ⅛ slice

Thin Pizza Crust

2 cups flour
1 teaspoon xanthan gum
1 teaspoon sugar
1 teaspoon salt
1 teaspoon baking powder
1 tablespoon oil
1 cup milk

Olive oil

Preheat the oven to 350° and grease a large pizza pan. Mix all ingredients into a very stiff dough. On a well-floured piece of plastic wrap, roll the dough out to fit the size of the pizza pan, sprinkling flour on the dough as well. Use the plastic wrap to transfer the crust to the pan. Bake 8 minutes.

Remove the crust from the pan. Grease the pan well with olive oil and place the pan back in the oven. Do not leave it in the oven for more than 5 minutes or the oil will burn. Top the pizza with desired toppings. Remove the hot pan from the oven, and slide the pizza onto it. Bake 15-20 minutes until the cheese is melted.

Total carbs 205g
About 25g carbs per ⅛ slice

Notes:

Notes:

Breakfast

Amish Breakfast Casserole

½ pound ham, cubed
½ cup onion, chopped
6 eggs
2 cups frozen cubed hash brown potatoes, thawed
1 cup shredded cheddar cheese
¾ cup cottage cheese
½ cup shredded Swiss cheese
1½ teaspoons salt
½ teaspoon pepper
Cayenne pepper to taste

Preheat the oven to 350° and grease a 2.5 quart casserole dish, or 9x9 pan. In a large skillet cook the ham and onions until the onions are tender. In a medium bowl, combine the remaining ingredients. Stir into the skillet just until mixed, then transfer it all to the prepared pan. Bake for 35-40 minutes.

Crumbled bacon or cooked, cut up sausage can be substituted for the ham.

Total carbs 60g

Berry Clafouti

(A bit like a thick crepe with berries on top)

1½ cups fresh blueberries and raspberries
2 teaspoons flour

3 eggs
1 cup milk
⅔ cup flour

¼ cup sugar
¼ teaspoon xanthan gum
1½ teaspoons vanilla
¼ teaspoon salt

Powdered sugar (optional)

Preheat the oven to 350° and grease a 2.5 quart baking dish. In a small bowl, toss the berries with the flour until they are evenly coated. Arrange the berries in the bottom of the dish and set aside.

In a medium bowl, whisk together the eggs through salt. Pour over the berries. Bake for about 50 minutes until it is puffed, golden brown, and set in the center. Serve warm with an optional dusting of powdered sugar on top.

Total carbs 179g
About 30g carbs for a ⅙ piece

Cinnamon Scones

2 ⅓ cups flour
⅔ cup sugar
4 teaspoons baking powder
1½ teaspoons xanthan gum
1 teaspoon baking soda
1 teaspoon cinnamon
½ teaspoon salt

2 eggs
⅔ cup butter, melted
¼ cup milk

1 tablespoon cinnamon sugar

Heat the oven to 400° and grease two 9 inch pie plates. In a large bowl, mix all the dry ingredients, flour through salt. Add in the eggs, butter, and milk. Mix with an electric mixer until well blended.

Turn dough out onto an oiled surface and pat into two 1 inch thick circles with oiled hands. Cut each circles into 8 wedges and place 1 inch apart on a greased cookie sheet. Sprinkle with cinnamon sugar and bake 15-20 minutes. Makes 16 wedges.

Total carbs 365g
About 23g carbs per wedge

Crepes

2¼ cups flour
¼ cup sugar
¼ teaspoon salt
5 eggs
3 cups milk
3 tablespoons butter, melted

Butter for the pan

Fruit filling:
2 cups berries
¼ cup flour
½ cup sugar
¼ cup water

Place all the ingredients in a large bowl and beat with a mixer until the batter is smooth. Place a small frying pan (or two) on the stove over medium-high heat and melt a little butter in the bottom. Pour just enough batter into the pan to cover the bottom. Swirl the pan to spread the batter to the edges. Cook for about a minute or so, and then flip the crepe over. Cook on the other side for another minute, or until the crepe is golden on both sides.

Keep warm in the oven while you finish cooking the rest of the crepes. Serve with warm fruit filling and/or syrup. Makes about 20 crepes.

For the fruit filling, put all ingredients in a small sauce pan. Mix, and cook over medium-high heat until bubbly and thickened.

Total carbs 325g
About 17g carbs per crepe without filling
Fruit Filling: About 10g carbs per tablespoon.

Crunchy Granola

½ cup brown sugar
½ cup butter, melted
¼ teaspoon salt
1 tablespoon honey
½ teaspoon vanilla

6 cups GF oats
½ cup sliced almonds
½ cup sunflower seeds
½ cup flaked coconut

Raisins, dried cranberries or other dried fruit - be creative

Preheat the oven to 350°. Line 2 large cookie sheets with foil and grease the foil. In a large bowl, mix the sugar, butter, salt, honey, and vanilla. Stir in the oats, almonds, sunflower seeds, and coconut. Spread the mixture out on the cookie sheets and bake for about 10-15 minutes, stirring frequently until golden brown. Allow to cool and add any dried fruit you might want in your granola.

Total carbs 470g without any extras added
About 30g carbs per ½ cup

Doughnut Balls

Dough:
1 tablespoon active dry yeast
⅓ cup warm water
⅓ cup sugar

1¼ cups flour
¼ teaspoon salt
½ teaspoon xanthan gum
3 tablespoons sour cream
1 egg

2-3 tablespoons flour
Oil for frying

Glaze:
¾ cup powdered sugar
1 tablespoon maple syrup
1 tablespoon water

Preheat the oven to warm. In a small bowl, combine the yeast, warm water, and sugar. Set aside and let rise. In a large bowl combine the flour, salt, and xanthan gum. Add the sour cream, egg, and yeast mixture. Using a whisk, beat until well blended. Turn the oven off, and put the bowl in the warm oven to rise for one hour or until double in size.

Punch the dough down. Allow to rise for 20 minutes more. Meanwhile, combine the powdered sugar, maple syrup, and water for the glaze and set aside. Place 2 inches of oil in a medium sauce pan and heat over medium to medium-high heat. When the oil is hot enough for a drop of water to sizzle, use a large spoon dipped in the hot oil to scoop out 1 inch balls of dough. Drop them into the hot oil.

Fry the dough balls, 5-6 at a time, for about 2 minutes on each side or until golden brown. Drain on paper towels and allow to cool a little. Roll the doughnut balls in the glaze, placing them on a cooling rack over a cookie sheet. Makes about 24 doughnut balls.

Total carbs 155g without the glaze
About 10g carbs per doughnut hole with the glaze

Fruit Swirl Coffee Cake

Cake:
4 eggs
¾ cup milk
½ cup butter, melted
2 teaspoons vanilla
3 cups GF store-bought baking mix
⅔ cup sugar

1 - 21 ounce can fruit pie filling (any flavor)

Glaze:
1 cup powdered sugar
2 tablespoons milk

Preheat the oven to 375°. Grease a cookie sheet with raised edges. In a large bowl, mix the cake ingredients until well blended. Spread ⅔ of the batter onto the cookie sheet. Spread the pie filling evenly over the batter. Drop the remaining batter in spoonfuls onto the pie filling. Bake 20-25 minutes. In a small bowl, mix the powdered sugar and milk and set aside. Allow the cake to cool slightly before drizzling the glaze on the top. Serve warm or cool.

Total carbs 264g
About 41g carbs per serving

Funnel Cakes

Oil for frying

1½ cups milk
2 eggs
2 cups flour
¼ cup sugar
1 teaspoon baking powder
½ teaspoon cinnamon
½ teaspoon salt
½ teaspoon xanthan gum

¾ cup powdered sugar

In a deep skillet heat 1 inch of oil until a drop of water sizzles.

While the oil is heating, beat the milk and eggs together in a large bowl. Add the remaining ingredients except powdered sugar and mix well. The batter should be smooth. Cover the bottom of a funnel with one finger while filling it with batter. Pour the batter out of the small end of the funnel into the oil, starting at the center and using a swirling motion to make a 5-6 inch round. Fry on both sides until it is golden brown. Drain on a paper towel and sprinkle with powdered sugar. Serve warm.

Total carbs 240g

Grandma Stime's Lefse

(Traditional Norwegian fare and the best breakfast of the year. Amazing hot off the grill!!)

5 pounds potatoes
1 heaping tablespoon salt
1 heaping tablespoon sugar
½ cup oil
½ cup milk

2 rounded cups flour
Butter
White sugar or brown sugar

Peel, and slice the potatoes, making sure you remove all the eyes. Cook them in a large pot of boiling water. When the potatoes are very soft, about ½ hour, drain them. Place in a large bowl, adding the salt, sugar, oil, and milk to the potatoes. Beat them for five minutes with an electric mixer. You need to get <u>all</u> the lumps out.

Place the potatoes in a 9x13 cake pan, cover and refrigerate overnight. In the morning, add 1 rounded cup of flour to half the potatoes in a large bowl. Mix until well incorporated. Dump the potatoes out onto a floured surface and shape into a log about 3 inches in diameter. Repeat with the other half when the first is done. Keep it refrigerated until then.

Place a large, flat skillet over medium heat. Cut the log into ½ inch slices and on a very well-floured, cloth surface, roll the slice out until it is extremely thin - about ⅛ inch. Make sure your rolling pin is covered with cloth and is well floured as well.

Using a spatula or lefse stick, carefully move the rolled out potato to the hot, dry skillet. Cook for a minute or so on one side, and then flip and cook on the other side until it's lightly browned. Place it on a towel to cool, or eat it quickly before anyone else gets it. Serve buttered with a sprinkle of white or brown sugar.

Total carbs 580g
About 15g carbs per round without sugar

Overnight Danish Pastries

1 tablespoon yeast
¼ cup warm water
2½ cups flour
⅓ cup sugar
1 teaspoon salt
½ teaspoon xanthan gum
½ cup butter
1 egg
½ cup milk

Jam or preserves

Powdered Sugar Glaze:
1½ cups powdered sugar
2 teaspoons butter
½ teaspoon vanilla
2-3 tablespoons milk

In a large bowl, dissolve the yeast in the warm water. Mix in the flour, sugar, and salt. Cut the butter into the mixture with a pastry cutter until it resembles coarse crumbs. Add the egg and milk until the mixture is a soft dough. Add a little more flour if necessary. Cover the mixture and refrigerate for at least 8 hours, but no more than 24 hours.

Lightly grease a large cookie sheet. Dump the cool dough onto a well-floured surface. Don't punch down. With floured hands, gently shape the dough into a 12x7 inch rectangle. Cut the dough into 12 one inch strips. Roll each strip gently into a rope and then connect the ends to form an oval. Gently pick up the loop, twist it into a figure eight, and place it on the cookie sheet. Repeat this with each strip, placing twists about 2 inches apart on the sheet.

Allow to rise in a warm place for 15-20 minutes, or until the loops are filled in. Preheat the oven to 350 °. In a small bowl, mix the glaze ingredients and set aside. Once the pastries have risen, place a teaspoon of jam or preserves in the center of each loop and bake for 15 minutes or until light brown. Cool and drizzle with powdered sugar glaze. Makes 12 pastries.

Total carbs 595g with glaze and jam
About 49g carbs per pastry

Pancakes

3 eggs
1½ cups flour
1 cup milk
1 tablespoon sugar
3 tablespoons oil
4½ teaspoons baking powder
¾ teaspoon xanthan gum
¼ teaspoon salt

Butter to grease the pan

In a large bowl, whisk together all the ingredients until smooth. Let the batter stand for a minute or two to thicken. Place a griddle or large frying pan on the stove over medium to medium-high heat. Grease the griddle with the butter.

Using a measuring cup, pour the batter onto the hot griddle or pan. Cook until bubbly in the middle and slightly cooked on the edges. Flip and cook until golden brown on the other side. Makes about sixteen 4-inch pancakes.

Total carbs 180g
About 12g carbs per pancake without syrup

Quick Danish Pastries

2 cups flour
2 tablespoons sugar
5 teaspoons baking powder
1 teaspoon xanthan gum
¼ teaspoon salt
½ teaspoon almond extract
¾ cup milk
¼ cup butter

¼ cup jam

Glaze:
⅔ cup powdered sugar
2 tablespoons milk
½ teaspoon vanilla extract

Preheat the oven to 400° and grease a cookie sheet. In a large bowl, mix the dry ingredients. Cut the butter into the dry ingredients until it forms coarse crumbs. Add the almond extract and milk and mix well. Place the dough by rounded tablespoons onto the cookie sheet. Make a dent in the center of each ball of dough and place a teaspoon of jam in it. Bake for 12-15 minutes. In a small bowl, mix the glaze ingredients and set aside. Drizzle with glaze when the pastries have cooled a little.

Total carbs 430g

Waffles

2 cups flour
2½ teaspoons baking powder
1 teaspoon salt
2 tablespoons sugar
⅓ cup oil
2 eggs
1½ cups milk

In a large bowl, mix all the ingredients with a whisk. Pour the batter into a hot, greased waffle iron using about ½ cup for each waffle, depending on the size of the waffle iron. Stir batter well before each waffle. Batter should be fairly runny. Add a little more milk if necessary, especially toward the end. Makes about 12 waffles.

Total carbs 265g
About 22g carbs per waffle without syrup

Homemade Maple Syrup

1 cup sugar
½ cup water
1 teaspoon maple extract

Place all ingredients in a medium sauce pan and heat just until boiling.

Total carbs 200g
About 15g carbs per tablespoon

Notes:

Notes:

Sweet Muffins

❧❧ ❖ ❧❧

Applesauce Oat Muffins

1¼ cups flour
½ cup GF quick oats
½ cup brown sugar
1½ teaspoons baking powder
½ teaspoon xanthan gum
¼ teaspoon cinnamon
¼ teaspoon salt
1 egg
¾ cup applesauce
¼ cup butter, melted

Topping:
2 tablespoons brown sugar
¼ cup GF oats

Preheat the oven to 350°. Grease a standard muffin tin, or line it with papers. In a medium bowl, mix all ingredients well with a whisk and spoon into the muffin tin. Top each muffin with ½ teaspoon brown sugar and a sprinkle of oats. Bake for 15-20 minutes. Makes about 12 muffins.

Total carbs 300g
About 25g carbs per muffin

Banana Bread

1 cup sugar
½ cup butter, softened
3 eggs
3-4 ripe bananas, mashed
½ cup milk
1 teaspoon vanilla
2½ cups flour
2 teaspoons egg replacer
1 teaspoon baking soda
1 teaspoon xanthan gum
1 teaspoon salt
1 cup chopped nuts, ½ cup raisins and/or ½ cup coconut if desired

Preheat the oven to 350° and grease 2 loaf pans well. In a large bowl, mix all the ingredients except nuts, raisins, and coconut until well blended. Add nuts, raisins, and coconut if desired. Pour into the prepared pans and bake for 35- 40 minutes. Cool on racks before cutting.

Total carbs 536g - without raisins or coconut
About 268g carbs per loaf
About 20g carbs per slice (14 slices per loaf)
Add 4g carbs per slice if you add raisins or coconut

Banana Nut Muffins

1½ cups flour
½ cup sugar
1½ teaspoons baking powder
⅓ teaspoon salt
½ teaspoon xanthan gum
2 eggs
¼ cup milk
¼ cup butter, melted
1 ripe banana, mashed
¼ cup walnuts, chopped

Preheat the oven to 350°. Grease a standard muffin tin or line it with papers. In a medium bowl, mix the dry ingredients, flour through xanthan gum. Add the remaining ingredients except the nuts and mix well. Fold in the nuts and spoon into the prepared pan. Bake for 15-20 minutes. Makes about 12 muffins.

Total carbs 284g
About 24g carbs per muffin

Blueberry Muffins

1½ cups flour
¾ teaspoon xanthan gum
1½ teaspoons baking powder
½ teaspoon salt
½ cup sugar
2 eggs
¼ cup butter, melted
⅔ cup milk
1 cup frozen blueberries

Preheat the oven to 350° and grease a standard muffin tin or line it with papers. Mix all the ingredients except the blueberries in a medium bowl with a whisk. Fold in the frozen blueberries. Spoon the batter into the prepared muffin tin and bake for 15-20 minutes. Makes about 12 muffins.

Total carbs 276g
About 23g carbs per muffin

Bomber Bran Muffins

1 cup flour
¼ cup rice bran
¼ cup flaxseed meal
¼ cup hazelnut meal *or* almond meal
¼ cup sugar
½ teaspoon xanthan gum
1 teaspoon baking powder
½ teaspoon salt
3 tablespoons molasses
¼ cup butter, melted
½ cup milk
2 eggs
½ cup raisins

Preheat the oven to 350°. Grease a standard muffin tin or line it with papers. Mix the dry ingredients in a medium bowl, flour through salt. Add the remaining ingredients. Mix well and spoon the batter into the prepared muffin tin. Bake for 15–20 minutes. Makes about 12 muffins.

Total carbs 360g
About 30g carbs per muffin

Caramel Nut Muffins

"Topping":
6 tablespoons butter, melted
½ cup brown sugar
½ cup chopped pecans *or* walnuts

Muffins:
1½ cups flour
¼ cup sugar

1½ teaspoons baking powder
⅓ teaspoon salt
½ teaspoon xanthan gum
½ teaspoon cinnamon
2 eggs
⅓ cup milk
¼ cup brown sugar
¼ cup butter, melted

Preheat the oven to 350° and spray a standard muffin tin well with cooking spray. Don't use paper liners. In a small bowl, mix the butter, brown sugar, and nuts. Divide evenly among the muffin cups. In a large bowl, mix the dry ingredients, flour through cinnamon.

Add the remaining ingredients. Mix together well and spoon the batter into a prepared muffin tin. Bake for 15–20 minutes. Turn the muffin tin over onto a cookie sheet and allow to cool for 2-3 minutes covered with the muffin tin. Makes about 12 muffins.

Total carbs 375g
About 31g carbs per muffin

Carrot Muffins

½ cup mayonnaise
½ cup plain yogurt
¾ cup sugar
3 eggs
2¼ cups flour
¾ teaspoon xanthan gum
2 teaspoons baking powder
1 teaspoon baking soda
1 teaspoon egg replacer

1 teaspoon cinnamon
1 teaspoon nutmeg
½ teaspoon salt

2 cups grated carrot
1 cup walnuts, chopped
½ cup raisins

Preheat the oven to 350°. Grease two standard muffin tins, or line them with papers. Prepare carrots and walnuts.

In a large bowl, beat the mayonnaise, yogurt, and sugar until smooth. Beat in eggs one at a time. Add the dry ingredients, flour through salt, and beat until smooth. Stir in the carrots, walnuts, and raisins. Spoon the batter into the prepared muffin tin and bake for 20-25 minutes. Makes about 18 muffins. Frost with cream cheese frosting if desired.

1 cup of finely chopped apple can be substituted for 1 cup of the carrots.

Total carbs 400g
About 23g carbs per muffin without frosting

Cranberry Muffins

1½ cups flour
¼ teaspoon xanthan gum
¾ teaspoon baking powder
1 teaspoon baking soda
½ teaspoon salt
⅓ cup sugar

2 eggs
6 tablespoons butter, melted
¾ cup milk
½ cup dried cranberries

Preheat the oven to 350°. Grease a standard muffin tin or line it with papers. Mix the dry ingredients in a large bowl, flour through sugar. Add remaining ingredients to the center of the bowl and mix well. Spoon into the prepared muffin tin and bake 15-20 minutes. Makes about 12 muffins.

Total carbs 275g
About 23g carbs per muffin

Honey Muffins

1½ cups flour
¼ cup sugar
1½ teaspoons baking powder
⅓ teaspoon salt
½ teaspoon xanthan gum
2 eggs
⅓ cup milk
¼ cup honey
¼ cup butter, melted

Preheat the oven to 350°. Grease a standard muffin tin or line it with papers. Mix the dry ingredients in a medium bowl, flour through xanthan gum. Add the remaining ingredients and mix well. Spoon into the prepared pan and bake for 15-20 minutes. Serve with butter. Makes about 12 muffins.

Total carbs 275g
About 23g carbs per muffin

Lemon Slice Muffins

2 lemons

2 tablespoons lemon zest
1 tablespoon water
¼ cup sugar
6 tablespoons butter

¼ cup sugar - divided

2 cups flour
¼ cup sugar
2 teaspoons baking powder
1 teaspoon egg replacer
1 teaspoon xanthan gum
½ teaspoon salt
2 eggs
¾ cup milk

Preheat the oven to 400° and grease a standard muffin tin. Don't use muffin papers. Finely grate the zest from the lemons, removing only the bright yellow part of the peel. Combine the zest, the water, and the ¼ cup of sugar in a small sauce pan. Cook on medium-high heat until the sugar is dissolved. Remove from heat and add the butter. Stir until the butter is melted and set aside.

Remove and discard the remaining peel from the lemons. Cut the lemons crosswise into very thin slices, about ¼ inch. You will need 12 slices. Discard the seeds. Put 1 teaspoon of sugar in the bottom of each muffin cup and place a lemon slice on top.

In a medium bowl, mix all the dry ingredients, flour through salt. Add the eggs, milk, and the lemon zest mixture. Stir just until blended. Spoon the batter into the prepared muffin tin and bake for 15-20 minutes. Immediately invert the muffin tin onto a cooling rack or cookie sheet. Cool for 5 minutes covered with the muffin tin, and then gently lift the tin. The muffins should fall out. Makes 12 muffins.

Total carbs 315g
About 26g carbs per muffin

Maple Walnut Muffins

1½ cups flour
½ teaspoon xanthan gum
1½ teaspoons baking powder
½ teaspoon salt
⅓ cup brown sugar
⅓ cup maple syrup
2 eggs
6 tablespoons butter, melted
⅓ cup milk
¼ cup walnuts, chopped

Preheat the oven to 350°. Grease a standard muffin tin or line it with papers. In a medium bowl, mix all the ingredients except walnuts until blended. Fold in the walnuts. Spoon the batter into the prepared muffin tin. Bake for 15-20 minutes. Makes about 12 muffins.

Total carbs 300g
About 25g carbs per muffin

Orange Yogurt Muffins

Zest of 1 large orange
¼ cup sugar
2 tablespoons water
4 tablespoons butter

½ cup flour
¼ cup sugar
1 teaspoon baking powder
1 teaspoon egg replacer
¼ teaspoon xanthan gum
½ teaspoon salt

2 eggs
1 cup plain yogurt
¼ cup milk

Streusel Topping:
¼ cup brown sugar
¼ cup pecans, finely chopped
2 tablespoons butter
2 tablespoons flour
½ teaspoon orange zest

Preheat the oven to 350°. Grease a standard muffin tin or line it with papers. Finely grate the zest from the orange. Only remove the bright orange part of the peel. Reserve ½ teaspoon of zest for the topping. Combine the remaining zest, sugar, and the water in a small sauce pan. Cook over medium-high heat until the sugar is dissolved. Remove from heat and add the butter. Stir until the butter is melted.

In a medium bowl, mix all the dry ingredients, flour through salt. Add the eggs, yogurt, milk, and the orange zest mixture. Stir until blended. Spoon the batter into prepared muffin tins.

With a pastry cutter, mix the streusel topping ingredients together in a small bowl and sprinkle on top of the muffins. Bake for 15-20 minutes. Makes about 12 muffins.

Total carbs 320g
About 27g carbs per muffin

Poppy Seed Muffins

1½ cups flour
¾ cup sugar
1 teaspoon egg replacer
¾ teaspoon xanthan gum
1 teaspoon baking powder
¼ teaspoon salt
1½ tablespoons poppy seeds
½ cup butter
⅔ cup milk
¾ teaspoon almond extract
3 eggs

Preheat the oven to 350°. Grease a standard muffin tin or line it with papers. In a medium bowl, beat all ingredients until well blended. Spoon the batter into the muffin tin and bake for 15-20 minutes. Makes about 16 muffins.

Total carbs 310g
About 20g carbs per muffin

Pumpkin Bread

¾ cup canned pumpkin
2 eggs
¾ cup brown sugar
¼ cup butter
3 tablespoons milk

1½ cups flour
¼ teaspoon baking soda

1 teaspoon baking powder
½ teaspoon salt
1 teaspoon xanthan gum
½ teaspoon cinnamon
¼ teaspoon nutmeg
Pinch of cloves
½ cup raisins
½ cup walnuts, chopped (optional)

Preheat the oven to 350° and grease a standard loaf pan. In a large bowl combine wet ingredients, pumpkin through milk. Add the remaining ingredients and mix well.

Pour the batter into the prepared pan and bake for 40-45 minutes. Allow the bread to cool for 5 minutes in the pan before removing to a cooling rack. Makes one loaf About 14 slices.

Total carbs 368g
About 26g carbs per slice

Strawberry Rhubarb Muffins

1½ cups flour
½ cup sugar
1½ teaspoons baking powder
½ teaspoon xanthan gum
⅓ teaspoon salt

2 eggs
⅓ cup milk
¼ cup honey
¼ cup butter, melted

¾ cup rhubarb, minced
½ cup strawberries, cut into chunks

Preheat the oven to 350°. Grease a standard muffin tin or line it with papers. Mix the dry ingredients in a medium bowl, flour through salt. Add remaining ingredients except rhubarb and strawberries and mix well. Fold in the rhubarb and strawberries. Spoon into the prepared pan and bake 15-20 minutes. Serve with butter. Makes about 12 muffins.

Total carbs 300g
About 25g carbs per muffin

Zucchini Bread

3 cups zucchini, shredded
1¼ cups sugar
⅔ cup oil
2 teaspoons vanilla
4 eggs
3 cups flour
½ cup milk
2½ teaspoons baking powder

1 teaspoon xanthan gum
1 teaspoon egg replacer
1 teaspoon salt
1 teaspoon cinnamon
½ teaspoon cloves

½ cup nuts, chopped (optional)
½ cup raisins (optional)

Preheat the oven to 350° and grease two standard loaf pans. Mix all the ingredients together in a large bowl until well blended. Pour half the batter into each loaf pan, and bake for 40-50 minutes or until done. Remove from the pans and cool before slicing.

Total carbs without raisins 639g
About 23g carbs per slice (14 slices per loaf)
Total carbs with raisins 690g
About 25g carbs per slice,

Notes:

Notes:

Savory Muffins

Amazing Cheesy Muffins

Cooking oil spray
1½ cups flour
2 tablespoons sugar
½ teaspoon salt
1 teaspoon baking powder
½ teaspoon xanthan gum
1 tablespoon rosemary

¼ cup onion, minced
2 teaspoons garlic, crushed
2 eggs
1 cup milk
¼ cup butter, melted
1½ cups shredded mozzarella cheese
¼ cup grated parmesan cheese

Preheat the oven to 350°. Prepare a standard muffin tin with paper liners. Grease the paper liners well with cooking oil spray. (These like to stick!)

Mix the dry ingredients in a large bowl, flour through rosemary. Add remaining ingredients to center of the bowl and mix well. Spoon the batter into the prepared tin and bake for 15-20 minutes. Serve with butter. Makes about 12 muffins.

Total carbs 192g
About 16g carbs per muffin

Apple Cheddar Muffins

1½ cups flour
¼ cup GF oats
3 tablespoons sugar
2 teaspoons baking powder
½ teaspoon xanthan gum
½ teaspoon salt

½ cup milk
2 eggs
¼ cup butter, melted
1 large apple, finely chopped
¾ cup cheddar cheese, grated

Preheat the oven to 350°. Grease a standard muffin tin or line it with papers. In a large bowl mix the dry ingredients, flour through salt. Add the remaining ingredients and mix until blended. Spoon into the prepared muffin tin and bake for 15-20 minutes. Makes about 12 muffins.

Total carbs 234g
About 19g carbs per muffin

Baking Powder Biscuits

2 cups flour
5 teaspoons baking powder
1 teaspoon xanthan gum
¼ teaspoon salt
¼ cup butter
¾ cup milk

Preheat the oven to 350° and grease a cookie sheet. Cut the butter into the dry ingredients in a medium bowl. Add the milk and mix until it's well blended. Place the dough in 3 inch mounds on the cookie sheet or roll out on a floured surface and cut into round biscuits. Bake for 12-15 minutes.

Total carbs 210g

Boston Brown Bread

1 cup flour
½ cup corn meal
¼ cup flax seed meal
1½ teaspoons baking powder
½ teaspoon xanthan gum
¼ teaspoon salt

2 eggs
⅓ cup milk
⅓ cup molasses
2 tablespoons brown sugar
1 tablespoon oil
3 tablespoons walnuts, chopped
3 tablespoons raisins

Preheat the oven to 350° and grease a standard loaf pan or standard muffin tin. Mix the dry ingredients, flour through salt, in a large bowl. Add the remaining ingredients and mix well with a whisk. Pour the batter into the prepared pan and bake for 35-40 minutes for the loaf pan, 15-20 minutes for muffins. Serve with softened cream cheese if desired. Makes one loaf. About 14 slices or 12 muffins.

Total carbs 310g
About 22g carbs per slice
About 26g carbs per muffin

Corn Bread

¾ cup flour
½ cup corn meal
¼ cup almond flour
¼ cup sugar
1½ teaspoons baking powder
½ teaspoon xanthan gum
¼ teaspoon salt
¾ cup milk
5 tablespoons butter, melted
2 eggs

Preheat the oven to 350°. Grease a standard muffin tin or an 8 inch cake pan. In a medium bowl, mix all the ingredients. Pour the batter into the prepared pan. Bake for 15-20 minutes. Makes about 12 muffins.

Total carbs 190g
About 16g carbs per muffin
About 24g carbs for a ⅛ piece

❖ Fried Corn Bread Medallions

Skip the butter. Place **2 tablespoons oil** in a frying pan and add the batter in spoonfuls. Fry several minutes on each side until cooked through. It will take several batches to cook all the batter. Add more oil to the pan for each batch, if needed.

Cracked Pepper Muffins

1½ cups flour
2 tablespoons sugar
2 teaspoons baking powder
½ teaspoon xanthan gum
½ teaspoon coarsely ground black pepper
¼ teaspoon salt
1 egg
¾ cup milk
2 tablespoons oil
1 cup shredded cheddar cheese

Preheat the oven to 350°. Grease a standard muffin tin or line it with papers. Mix all the dry ingredients in a medium bowl until well blended. Spoon the batter into the muffin cups and bake for 15-20 minutes. Makes about 12 muffins.

Total carbs 190g
About 16g carbs per muffin

Savory Herb Muffins

1½ cups flour
3 tablespoons grated parmesan cheese
2 tablespoons sugar
1 tablespoon Italian seasonings
2 teaspoons baking powder
½ teaspoon xanthan gum
½ teaspoon salt

2 eggs
½ cup milk
½ cup olive oil

Garlic Butter:
¼ cup butter, softened
½ teaspoon garlic salt

Preheat the oven to 350°. Grease a standard muffin tin or line it with papers. Mix the dry ingredients in a large bowl, flour through salt. Add remaining ingredients and mix well. Spoon into the prepared pan and bake 15-20 minutes. Serve with garlic butter.

Total carbs 186g
About 15g carbs per muffin

Notes:

Cakes

Almond Apricot Coffee Cake

¼ cup water
⅓ cup dried apricots, chopped

Crumb Topping:
½ cup flour
⅓ cup powdered sugar
Pinch of salt
3 tablespoons butter
½ teaspoon vanilla

Cake:
1½ cups flour
¾ cup sugar
1½ teaspoons baking powder
1 teaspoon grated orange peel
1 teaspoon salt
1 teaspoon egg replacer
¾ teaspoon xanthan gum
3 eggs
¼ cup oil
¼ cup orange juice
⅓ cup slivered almonds

Preheat the oven to 350° and grease a 9x9 baking pan. In a small sauce pan, bring the water and apricots to a boil. Remove from the heat and set aside. In a small bowl, mix the crumb topping ingredients with a pastry cutter until coarse crumbs form and set aside.

In a large bowl, combine all the cake ingredients except the almonds. Beat until well blended. Fold in the almonds and the apricots, including 2 tablespoons of the cooking liquid if the batter is on the thicker side. Pour the batter into the pan and sprinkle with the crumb topping. Bake for 35-40 minutes or until done.

Total carbs 480g
About 53g carbs per ⅑ piece

Almond Joy Cake

Streusel Topping:
⅔ cup flour
½ cup sugar
½ cup shredded coconut
¼ cup butter
½ cup mini chocolate chips

Cake:
1 cup butter, softened
¾ cup brown sugar
3 eggs

1 cup sour cream
1 teaspoon vanilla
⅓ teaspoon almond extract

1¾ cups flour
½ cup almond flour
1 teaspoon egg replacer
1 teaspoon baking powder
¼ teaspoon xanthan gum
¼ teaspoon salt

Preheat the oven to 350° and grease a 9x13 cake pan. In a medium bowl, mix the flour, sugar, and coconut. Cut the butter into the dry ingredients with a pastry cutter. Add the chocolate chips, mix well and set aside.

In a large bowl, cream the butter and brown sugar until fluffy. Add the eggs, sour cream, vanilla, and almond extract and mix. Mix in the dry ingredients, flour through salt.

Pour into the prepared pan. Sprinkle the streusel topping over the batter and bake for 30-35 minutes.

Total carbs 551g

Angel Food Sponge Cake
(Great for strawberry shortcake)

3 eggs, divided
¾ cup sugar
1½ tablespoons lemon juice
4 tablespoons boiling water
¼ teaspoon salt
⅔ cup tapioca starch (scant)

Preheat the oven to 300°. Grease a 9x9 pan. Separate the eggs. Place the yolks in a large bowl and the whites in a small bowl. Beat the egg whites until stiff peaks form and then set aside. Beat the egg yolks until light and fluffy. Add the sugar to the egg yolks and beat on medium speed until well incorporated.

Add the lemon juice, boiling water, and salt to the egg yolks and mix well. Add the tapioca starch by hand and then fold in the egg whites. Bake for 25 minutes, then increase the heat to 350° and bake for another 20 minutes, or until the cake is done.

This cake does dry out quickly. It's best eaten the first day, and the rest frozen for later use.

Total carbs 220g
About 25g carbs per ⅑ piece

Apple Cinnamon Coffee Cake

Apple Mixture:
3 cups apple, peeled, finely chopped
2 teaspoons cinnamon
¼ cup sugar

Crumb Topping:
4 tablespoons butter
½ cup flour
½ teaspoon cinnamon
¼ cup sugar

Cake:
½ cup butter
1 cup sugar
8 ounces cream cheese, softened
1 teaspoon vanilla
2 eggs
1¾ cups flour
½ teaspoon baking powder
1 teaspoon egg replacer
¼ teaspoon xanthan gum
¼ teaspoon salt

Preheat the oven to 350° and grease a 9x9 square baking pan for a taller cake, or a 9x13 pan for a shorter cake.

In a small bowl, toss the apples with the cinnamon and sugar and set aside. In a medium bowl, prepare the crumb topping by cutting the butter into the remaining ingredients until it resembles coarse crumbs. Set aside.

In a large bowl cream the butter and sugar until white and fluffy. Beat in the cream cheese and vanilla. Add eggs one at a time. Stir in the dry ingredients, flour through salt. Fold the apples into the batter. Spoon the batter into the prepared pan and sprinkle the crumb topping over the top. Bake for 40-50 minutes for 9x9 inch pan, 30-40 minutes for 9x13 inch pan.

Total carbs 640g
About 70g carbs per ⅑ piece, 53g carbs per 1/12 piece

Basic Cheesecake

2 cups boiling water

Crust:

2 cups finely crushed rice cereal
½ teaspoon ground cinnamon
6 tablespoons butter, melted

Filling:

16 ounces cream cheese, softened
3 eggs
¾ cup sugar
2 cups sour cream
1 teaspoon lemon zest
½ teaspoon vanilla extract

Preheat the oven to 325° and grease an 8-inch springform pan. Wrap the base of the pan in a double layer of foil. In a medium bowl combine the crust ingredients until well mixed. Pour them into the pan and press down firmly.

In a large bowl, beat the cream cheese on low speed for 1 minute until smooth and free of lumps. Add the eggs one at a time, and continue to beat gently until combined. Add the sugar slowly and mix until creamy. Mix in the sour cream, lemon zest, and vanilla.

Pour the filling into the crust-lined pan and smooth the top with a spatula. Place the springform pan in a large roasting pan. Pour the boiling water into the roasting pan until the water is about halfway up the sides of the cheesecake pan.

Bake for 45 minutes. The cheesecake should still jiggle slightly in the center. Let it cool in the pan for 30 minutes. Loosen the cheesecake from the sides of the pan by running a knife around the inside rim. Chill in the refrigerator for at least 4 hours.

Total carbs 220g
About 19g carbs per ¹⁄₁₂ piece

Carrot Cake

1 cup sugar
¾ cup coconut oil
4 eggs
3 cups shredded carrots

2 cups flour
1½ teaspoons ground cinnamon
1 teaspoon baking soda
1 teaspoon vanilla
½ teaspoon xanthan gum
½ teaspoon salt
¼ teaspoon ground nutmeg

1 cup nuts, chopped (optional)

Preheat the oven to 350°. Grease a 9x13 pan or two 8 inch round pans. Beat the sugar, oil, eggs, and carrots in a large bowl until well blended. Add the remaining ingredients except nuts and beat well. Fold in the nuts, if desired, and pour into the pan. Bake 35-40 minutes or until done. Frost with butter cream cheese frosting.

Total carbs 410g - without frosting

Cinnamon Roll Cake

Cake:
3 eggs
½ cup butter, softened
¾ cup sugar
1½ cups flour
¾ teaspoon xanthan gum
1 teaspoon baking powder
1 teaspoon egg replacer
¼ teaspoon salt
⅓ cup milk
¾ teaspoon vanilla

Topping:
½ cup butter, melted
1 cup brown sugar
1 tablespoon cinnamon
½ cup pecans, chopped

Glaze:
1 cup powdered sugar
1 tablespoon milk (scant)
1 teaspoon vanilla

Preheat the oven to 350° and grease a 9x13 pan. Mix all topping ingredients in a small bowl and set aside. In a large bowl, add all the cake ingredients and beat on high until well blended and fluffy. Pour into the pan.

Drop the topping over the cake in spoonfuls and using a knife, swirl it gently into the cake. Don't overmix. Bake 25-30 minutes. While the cake is baking, mix the glaze ingredients in a small bowl and set aside. Drizzle the glaze over the warm cake and serve.

Total carbs 590g

Flourless Chocolate Cake

1 cup butter
2⅔ cups semisweet chocolate chips
8 eggs
¼ cup sugar
1½ teaspoons vanilla
½ teaspoon salt

2 cups boiling water
Powdered sugar for garnish (optional)

Preheat the oven to 325°. Grease a 9-inch springform pan and line the bottom with wax paper. Cover the outside of the pan with a double layer of foil and set it in a roasting pan.

In a medium bowl, melt the butter in the microwave. Add the chocolate chips and melt in 30 second increments until just melted. Don't overcook.

In the bowl of a stand mixer, add the eggs, sugar, vanilla, and salt. Mix until almost double in size, 5-10 minutes. Gently fold the chocolate mixture into the egg mixture. Pour the batter into the springform pan. Add enough boiling water to the roasting pan to come half way up the springform pan. Bake for 40-50 minutes until the edges are set. Cool at room temperature and then refrigerate overnight.

Total carbs 300g
About 38g carbs per ⅛ slice

Gingerbread Cake with Caramel Sauce

Cake:
¼ cup butter, softened
½ cup brown sugar
¼ cup molasses
2 eggs
1½ cups flour
1½ teaspoons baking powder
1 teaspoon ground ginger
½ teaspoon cinnamon
½ teaspoon salt

½ teaspoon xanthan gum
¾ cup milk

Caramel sauce:
1 cup brown sugar
¾ cup water
2 tablespoons flour
Dash of salt
1 tablespoon butter
¼ teaspoon vanilla

Preheat the oven to 350° and prepare a 9x9 pan. In a medium bowl, beat all the cake ingredients until fluffy. Spread the batter in the pan and bake for 35-40 minutes.

While the cake is baking, bring the caramel sauce ingredients to a boil in a small sauce pan over medium-high heat. Cook until thickened. Cool slightly and serve drizzled over pieces of the warm cake.

Total carbs 310g for the cake
About 35g carbs for a ⅑ piece
Total carbs 225g for the caramel sauce
About 15g carbs per tablespoon

Ice Cream Roll Cake

4 eggs, separated
⅔ cup sugar, divided
¾ teaspoon vanilla
½ teaspoon cream of tartar
¼ teaspoon salt
1 teaspoon baking powder
¾ cup flour

Powdered sugar for dusting

Preheat the oven to 350°. Place wax paper on the bottom of a cookie sheet with ½ inch edges or a jelly roll pan and grease the paper. Separate the eggs. Put the egg yolks in a medium bowl and the whites in a small bowl. Beat the egg whites until frothy. Add ⅓ cup of the sugar, the vanilla, and the cream of tartar to the egg whites. Continue beating until stiff peaks form.

Beat the egg yolks until thick and fluffy. Add the remaining ⅓ cup sugar, salt, and baking powder, then gently fold in the egg white mixture. Fold the flour into the batter in small amounts. Pour the batter into the prepared pan and bake for 15-18 minutes.

Immediately invert the cake onto dish towel dusted with powdered sugar. Remove the wax paper. Roll the cake in the towel, starting from the short side, and making sure the towel separates the sections of cake. Allow the cake to cool. Unroll the cake and add a layer of ice cream. Reroll the cake without the towel. Wrap in foil and freeze. Dust the top with powdered sugar when you're ready to serve.

Total carbs 216g for cake without any filling
See ice cream container for additional carbs

Alternate fillings for the ice cream cake:

❖ **Whipped Cream and Fruit Filling:**

Layer cake with 1 inch of whipped cream and dot with fruit of your choice.

Carbs depend on the fruit used and the amount of sugar in the whipped cream

❖ **Jam and Cream Cheese Filling:**

Mix 8 ounces of softened cream cheese with ½ cup of jam, spread over cake.

110g carbs for cream cheese filling

❖ **Almond Joy Filling:**

2 cups whipped cream
2 cups shredded coconut
Pinch of salt
1½ cups slivered almonds, toasted
Chocolate syrup

In a medium bowl, mix the whipped cream, coconut, and salt. Spread over the cake followed by a layer of almonds and a drizzle of chocolate syrup.

144g carbs for almond joy filling

Lemon Pound Cake

Cake:
6 tablespoons butter, softened
¾ cup sugar
3 eggs
⅓ cup sour cream
1 teaspoon vanilla
2 teaspoons lemon zest
1½ cups flour
1 teaspoon baking powder
½ teaspoon salt
¼ teaspoon xanthan gum

Frosting:
1 cup powdered sugar
½ teaspoon lemon extract
1 tablespoon butter, softened
Just enough milk to make a thick frosting

Preheat the oven to 350° and grease a standard loaf pan. In a large bowl, beat the butter and sugar until creamy. Add the eggs, sour cream, vanilla, and zest, and beat well. Add the remaining ingredients and mix until well incorporated. Pour into the loaf pan and bake about 30-35 minutes or until done.

Make the frosting while the cake is cooking. Cool the cake for 5 minutes before removing from pan. Frost the cake once it's cool.

Total carbs 305g - without the frosting
About 22g carbs per slice
Total carbs 405g - with the frosting
About 29g carbs per slice

Lenora's Chocolate Cake

(A very good basic chocolate cake)

2 cups flour
1½ cups sugar
½ cup butter, softened
½ cup cocoa
2½ teaspoons baking powder
1 teaspoon salt
½ teaspoon xanthan gum
1 cup water

4 eggs
1 teaspoon vanilla

Preheat the oven to 350° and grease a 9x13 cake pan. In a large bowl, mix the first 8 ingredients, flour through water. Beat by hand with a spoon or whisk until smooth. Add the eggs and vanilla and stir by hand until well blended. Pour the batter into the pan. Bake for 30 minutes, allow to cool and frost with One Minute Chocolate Icing, if desired. This can be made into cupcakes as well.

Total carbs 500g carbs total - without the frosting

Pineapple Upside-Down Cake

¼ cup butter, melted
½ cup brown sugar
1 - 16 ounce can pineapple chunks, drained

1½ cups flour
¾ cup sugar
¼ cup butter
½ cup milk
1½ teaspoons baking powder
1 teaspoon egg replacer
½ teaspoon xanthan gum
½ teaspoon salt
2 eggs

Preheat the oven to 350°. Pour the melted butter into a 9x9 pan. Spread it over the bottom and sides to grease the pan. Add the brown sugar and spread evenly over the bottom of the pan then layer the pineapple on top of the sugar mixture. In a large bowl, beat the remaining ingredients until light and fluffy. Pour on top of the pineapple. Bake for 40-50 minutes. Invert immediately onto a plate.

Total carbs 458g
About 50g carbs per ⅑ piece

Upside-Down Cake Variations:

❖ Rhubarb Upside-Down Cake

Replace the pineapple with 1½ cups chopped rhubarb.

Total carbs 423g
About 47g carbs per ⅑ piece

❖ Berry Upside-Down Cake

Substitute 3 tablespoons granulated sugar for the brown sugar and spread 1½ cups blueberries, blackberries or raspberries on the bottom of the pan instead of the pineapple.

Total carbs 345g
About 39g carbs per ⅑ piece

Pumpkin Cheesecake

Crust:
1 cup GF rice cereal, finely crushed
¼ cup almond meal
1 tablespoon sugar
¼ teaspoon pumpkin pie spice
4 tablespoons butter, melted

Filling:
16 ounces cream cheese, softened
1 cup canned pumpkin
½ cup sugar
3 tablespoons flour
2 tablespoons maple syrup

⅓ teaspoon ginger
⅓ teaspoon cinnamon
⅓ teaspoon nutmeg
3 eggs, lightly beaten

Topping:
1 cup sour cream
3 tablespoons sugar
¼ teaspoon vanilla
¼ cup slices almonds

2 cups boiling water

Preheat the oven to 325°. In a small bowl, combine the cereal crumbs, almond meal, sugar, and pumpkin pie spice. Stir in the butter. Press into the bottom of a greased 8 inch springform pan. Bake for 10 minutes. Allow to cool. A nut crust can also be used.

In a large bowl, beat the cream cheese until smooth. Add the pumpkin, through spices, and beat until smooth. Add the eggs and beat on low speed until just combined. Securely wrap the bottom of the pan in a double thickness of foil. Pour the cream cheese mixture over the crust. Place the spring-form pan into a roasting pan and add boiling water to the roasting pan until it comes half way up the springform pan. Bake for 55-60 minutes or until the center is almost set.

In a small bowl, combine the sour cream, sugar, and vanilla. Spread over the hot cheesecake. Sprinkle with almonds. Bake 18-20 minutes longer or until the topping is set. Remove the pan from the water and cool 10 minutes on a wire rack. Carefully run a knife around edge of the pan and cool 1 hour longer. Refrigerate 3 hours or overnight.

Total carbs 285g - About 43g carbs for the crust

Pumpkin Spice Cake

4 eggs
1 cup sugar
1 cup oil
1 - 15 ounce can pumpkin

2 cups flour
2 teaspoons baking powder
1 teaspoon baking soda
½ teaspoon xanthan gum
1 teaspoon salt
2 teaspoons cinnamon
¼ teaspoon ginger
¼ teaspoon nutmeg

Preheat the oven to 350° and grease a 9x13 cake pan. In a large bowl, beat the eggs, sugar, oil, and pumpkin until well blended. Add the remaining ingredients, baking powder through nutmeg, and mix well. Pour into the prepared pan and bake for 30-35 minutes. Cool completely before frosting with cream cheese frosting, if desired.

Total carbs 335g - without frosting

Ross' Caramel Pecan Cake

Large Bundt Cake:

3 cups flour
1½ cups brown sugar
1½ teaspoons xanthan gum
2 teaspoons egg replacer
2 teaspoons baking powder
½ teaspoon salt
1 cup butter
¾ cup milk
1½ teaspoons vanilla
6 eggs

1 cup pecans, chopped
1 tablespoon powdered sugar

Smaller Cake (9x13 pan):

1½ cups flour
¾ cup brown sugar
¾ teaspoon xanthan gum
1 teaspoon baking powder
1 teaspoon egg replacer
¼ teaspoon salt
½ cup butter
⅓ cup milk
¾ teaspoon vanilla
3 eggs

½ cup pecans, chopped
½ tablespoon powdered sugar

Preheat the oven to 350°. Grease desired pan, bundt, 9x13 or muffin tin. Beat all the ingredients except the pecans and powdered sugar for 3 minutes. Fold in the pecans. Pour into the prepared pan. Bake 60-70 minutes for the bundt pan, 30-35 minutes for the 9x13 cake, 20-25 minutes for cupcakes. Cool the bundt cake 5 minutes before inverting onto cooling rack. Sprinkle with powdered sugar when cool. The smaller cake recipe makes about 15 cupcakes.

Bunt cake - Total carbs 546g
Smaller cake - Total carbs 248g
About 20g carbs per cupcake

Spice Cake

2 cups flour
1 cup sugar
2 teaspoons baking powder
1 teaspoon egg replacer
½ teaspoon xanthan gum
1 teaspoon cinnamon
½ teaspoon salt
¼ teaspoon nutmeg
¼ teaspoon cloves
¼ teaspoon ginger
1 cup milk
½ cup butter, softened
½ teaspoon vanilla
3 eggs

Preheat the oven to 350°. Grease a 9x13 pan or two standard muffin tins. In a large bowl, combine all ingredients and beat for 2-3 minutes, until light and fluffy. Pour into prepared pan and bake for 30-35 minutes. For cupcakes, bake for 20-25 minutes. Makes about 20 cupcakes. Frost with cream cheese frosting if desired.

Total carbs 312g

Yellow Cake

(Despite its uninspiring name, this is a very versatile and delicious recipe)

3 eggs, separated
½ cup butter
¾ cup sugar
1½ cups flour
¾ teaspoon xanthan gum
1 teaspoon baking powder
1 teaspoon egg replacer
¼ teaspoon salt
⅓ cup milk
¾ teaspoon vanilla

Preheat the oven to 350°. Grease the desired pan, muffin tin, two 9 inch rounds or a 9x13 pan. In a large bowl beat the butter and sugar until light and fluffy. Separate the eggs, with whites in a small bowl, and yolks in the big bowl with the butter mixture. Beat the egg whites until soft peaks form. Add all remaining ingredients except egg whites to the butter and beat on high until well blended. Fold in the egg whites. Pour into the prepared pan. Bake 15- 20 minutes for cupcakes, 20-25 minutes for two 9 inch rounds, and 25-30 minutes for a 9x13 pan.

Total carbs 300g
About 19g carbs per cupcake - without frosting

-Frostings-

Butter Cream Frosting

½ cup shortening
½ cup butter, softened
1 teaspoon vanilla
3 tablespoons milk
5 cups powdered sugar

Cream the shortening and butter in a large bowl. Add the vanilla and milk, then add the powdered sugar one cup at time until well blended and fluffy.

Total carbs 500g
About 15g carbs per tablespoon

Cream Cheese Butter Frosting

½ cup cream cheese, softened
½ cup butter, softened
1 teaspoon vanilla
3 tablespoons milk
5 cups powdered sugar

Cream the cream cheese and butter in a large bowl. Add the vanilla and milk, then add the sugar one cup at time until well blended and fluffy.

Total carbs 500g
About 15g carbs per tablespoon

Low Carb Frosting

2 ounces cream cheese, softened
½ teaspoon vanilla
3 tablespoons sugar
1 – 8 ounce tub whipped topping

In a large bowl, beat the cream cheese, vanilla, and sugar until light and fluffy. Fold in the whipped topping.

Total carbs 100g
About 5g carbs per tablespoon

Marshmallow Fondant

1 - 16 ounce package mini marshmallows

¼ cup water

1½ teaspoons vanilla

7 cups powdered sugar

1-2 cups powdered sugar

Food coloring of choice

Prepared cake

In a medium bowl, microwave the marshmallows in 30 second increments until melted. Place the marshmallows in the bowl of a stand mixer. Stir in the water, vanilla, and food coloring of choice if you want it colored. Mix until smooth. Add 7 cups of the powdered sugar, 1 cup at a time, until you have a thick, sticky dough.

Turn the dough out onto a surface covered with 1 cup of the remaining powdered sugar. Knead until the dough is smooth, pliable and no longer sticky. Add more powdered sugar if necessary. Cover in plastic wrap until ready to use.

Cover your cake with a thin layer of butter cream frosting. Allow to dry for 10-15 minutes. Using a paper towel, smooth the surface of the cake. Any lumps and bumps will show through the fondant.

Roll the fondant out on a surface well dusted with powdered sugar until it is very thin. Using a rolling pin, carefully pick it up and drape it over the cake. Using powdered hands, gently rub the fondant until it lays smooth on the cake. Cut away extra fondant and decorate as desired.

Fondant can be wrapped well and frozen until ready to use.

Carbs are difficult to figure out due to fondant thickness and the amount of scraps
About 15g carbs per tablespoon

One Minute Chocolate Frosting

1½ cups sugar
¼ cup butter
⅓ cup cocoa
⅓ cup milk
1 teaspoon vanilla

Bring all ingredients to a boil in a medium sauce pan over medium heat. Boil for <u>exactly</u> one minute. Remove from heat and partially cool before frosting the cake. (This frosting is a bit tricky. Cook it too long and it turns into fudge, not long enough and it's runny, but when it comes out right, it's outstanding!)

Total carbs 155g
About 15g carbs per tablespoon

Quick Chocolate Frosting

½ cup butter, melted
⅔ cup unsweetened cocoa
3 cups powdered sugar
⅓ cup milk
1 teaspoon vanilla

In a medium bowl, mix the butter with the remaining ingredients on low speed until smooth. Add a few more drops of milk if needed.

Total carbs 300g
About 15g carbs per tablespoon

Notes:

Notes:

_____
_____
_____
_____
_____
_____
_____
_____
_____
_____
_____
_____
_____
_____
_____
_____
_____
_____
_____
_____

Cookies

Blond Brownies

¼ cup butter, softened
¾ cup brown sugar
1 teaspoon vanilla
1 teaspoon baking powder
¼ teaspoon salt
½ teaspoon xanthan gum
2 eggs
1 cup flour
½ cup walnuts, chopped

Heat oven to 350° and grease a 9x9 inch pan. Beat all the ingredients with a mixer until the batter is smooth. Spread it in the prepared pan, and bake for 25 minutes. Makes 16 brownies.

Total carbs 200g
About 13g carbs per brownie

Brownie Cookies

½ cup butter
4 ounces unsweetened chocolate
    baking squares
1½ cups chocolate chips

4 large eggs
2 cups flour
1½ cups sugar

1½ teaspoons vanilla
¾ teaspoon xanthan gum
½ teaspoon baking powder
½ teaspoon salt

2 cups pecans, finely chopped
1½ cups chocolate chips

Preheat the oven to 350° and grease several cookie sheets. In a small microwave-safe bowl, cook the butter in the microwave for 30 seconds. Add the chocolate baking squares and chocolate chips and melt in the microwave using 30 second increments just until melted and smooth. Don't overcook. In a large bowl, beat the eggs, then add the dry ingredients, flour through salt. Mix well. Add the melted chocolate and mix again. Stir in the pecans and the remaining chocolate chips.

Drop by 1 inch spoonfuls of dough onto the prepared cookie sheets, about 2 inches apart. Bake for 10-12 minutes or until browned on the edges. Cool several minutes before transferring to a cooling rack.

Total carbs 964g
About 26g carbs per cookie

Caramel Cookies

1 cup butter, softened
1 cup brown sugar
2 tablespoons vanilla
2 eggs
1½ teaspoons baking powder
¾ teaspoon xanthan gum
2¼ cups flour
1½ cups pecans, finely chopped

Preheat the oven to 350° and grease several cookie sheets. In a large bowl, cream the butter and brown sugar. Add the vanilla and beat in the eggs. Add the baking powder, xanthan gum, and flour and mix well. Fold in the nuts and mix until well incorporated.

Drop by 1 inch spoonfuls of dough onto the prepared cookie sheets, about 2 inches apart. Bake for 8-10 minutes or until browned on the edges. Cool several minutes before transferring to a cooling rack.

Total carbs 350g
About 20g carbs per cookie

Caramel Truffles

4 tablespoons butter
1⅓ cups chocolate chips
¼ cup caramel topping

½ pound chocolate candy coating

Melt the butter in a medium microwave safe bowl. Add the chocolate chips and cook in the microwave in 30 second increments just until the chips are melted, stirring frequently. Add the caramel topping and mix well.

Place in fridge for 1 hour. Roll the cooled chocolate mixture into 1 inch balls and place on a cookie sheet covered in wax paper. Place in the freezer for 15 minutes. Melt the candy coating in the microwave using 30 second increments just until melted. Don't overcook. Dip the balls in the candy coating and place them on a new sheet of wax paper to cool.

About 15g carbs per truffle

Coconut No Bake Butter Balls

(Almost no carbs)

Cookies:
½ cup butter
½ cup coconut flour
½ cup unsweetened shredded coconut
¼ cup almond meal
3 packets stevia

Coating:
Shredded coconut

In a large bowl, mix all the cookie ingredients with a pastry cutter. Roll into balls, then roll the balls in the remaining shredded coconut. Keep in fridge or freezer.

About 1g carbs per cookie

Chocolate Cookie Balls

2 packages GF chocolate cookies with white cream filling-About 40 cookies
1 - 8 ounce package of cream cheese, softened
1 - 16 ounce package of vanilla candy coating

Crushed peppermints, nuts or sprinkles (optional)

In a gallon sized zipper bag, crush the cookies with a rolling pin in two batches until they are finely ground. Place them in a large bowl with the cream cheese. Using a pastry cutter, mix until well blended. Place in the fridge for 1 hour.

Roll the mixture into 1 inch balls and place on a cookie sheet lined with wax paper. Place the cookie sheet in the freezer for 15 minutes. Melt the candy coating in the microwave using 30 second increments just until melted. Don't overcook. Dip each ball in the candy coating and place on a new sheet of wax paper. Immediately add whatever decoration you want to the top and allow to cool.

About 15g carbs per ball

Chocolate Covered Cherries

30 maraschino cherries with stems
2 tablespoons butter, softened
1¼ cups powdered sugar
½ pound chocolate candy coating

Place the cherries on paper towels and pat dry. In a medium bowl, mix the butter and sugar until it forms a stiff paste. Using about 1 teaspoon of the paste, wrap each cherry. Place on a cookie sheet covered in wax paper and put in the fridge for 30 minutes.

Melt the candy coating in the microwave using 30 second increments just until melted. Don't overcook. Dip the cherries in the candy coating and place them on a new sheet of wax paper to cool. Place the cherries in a sealed container and allow to sit in a cool place for several weeks.

About 12g carbs per cherry

Chocolate Chip Cookies

½ cup butter, softened
1 cup brown sugar
3 tablespoons sugar
1 egg
2 teaspoons vanilla

2 cups flour
½ teaspoon baking soda
½ teaspoon baking powder
½ teaspoon xanthan gum
½ teaspoon salt
1½ cups chocolate chips

Preheat the oven to 350° and grease several cookie sheets. Beat the butter and sugars until creamy. Add the egg and vanilla and mix well.

Add the dry ingredients, flour through salt, and mix well. Stir in the chocolate chips. Drop 1 inch spoonfuls of the dough onto the cookie sheets about 2 inches apart and bake for 8-10 minutes. Cool several minutes on the cookie sheets before transferring to cooling racks.

Dough can be frozen for later use.

Total carbs 670g
About 15g carbs per cookie

Cream Cheese Sugar Cookies

(This is a large recipe that can be made into almost anything)

Basic Dough:
2 cups butter, softened
8 ounces cream cheese, softened
2 cups sugar
1 egg
1½ teaspoons vanilla
4 teaspoons xanthan gum
5 cups flour

Preheat the oven to 350° and grease several cookie sheets. In a large bowl, cream the butter until smooth. Add cream cheese and beat until fluffy. Add the remaining ingredients. Mix well, and refrigerate for at least 1 hour. Roll the dough out on a floured surface, cut it into desired shapes, and decorate with sprinkles. Or make the dough into one of the variations on following pages. Bake for 10-12 minutes. When cool, decorate with any type of frosting.

Wrap well and freeze any unused dough.

Total carbs 870g
About 10g carbs per 1½ inch cookie, undecorated

Cream Cheese Sugar Cookie Variations:

Chai Tea Eggnog Cookies

Use half of the basic dough. Add the contents of **1 chai tea bag, 2 tablespoons eggnog** and **3 tablespoons flour.** Roll the cookies into balls and then flatten. Bake at 350° for 10-12 minutes. Once cool, frost with **1 cup powdered sugar** mixed with ½ **teaspoon nutmeg** and **2 tablespoons eggnog**.

About 18g carbs per 1½ inch cookie

Cherry Chunk Cookies

Use half of the basic dough. Add ⅓ **cup maraschino cherries, finely chopped** and **3 tablespoons flour** or more to make a manageable dough. Roll into balls and bake at 350° for 10-12 minutes. Once they are cooled, dip half of each cookie in melted **chocolate candy coating**.

About 12g carbs per cookie

Gingerbread Pinwheels

Use half of the basic dough. Divide in half again. Leave one quarter plain, to the other quarter, add **1 teaspoon ground ginger, 1 teaspoon cinnamon, 2 tablespoons molasses,** and **3 tablespoons flour.**

Roll both batches of dough into rectangles about ¼ inches thick on pieces of plastic wrap. Place the gingerbread dough on top of the plain dough. Starting on the long side and using the plastic wrap as a guide, roll the double-layered dough into a log. Cut the log into ¼ inch thick slices. Bake at 350° for 10-12 minutes.

About 12g carbs per 1½ inch cookie

Macaroons

Use half of the basic dough. **Add 1 cup shredded coconut.** Roll the dough into balls and then roll each ball in additional **shredded coconut** to coat. Bake at 350° for 15 minutes. Press a chocolate kiss into the top as soon as they come out of the oven if desired.

About 12g carbs for a 1½ inch cookie without the chocolate kiss
About 17 g carbs with the chocolate kiss

Orange Sandwiches

Use half of the basic dough. Add **1 tablespoon grated orange zest** and ½ **teaspoon orange extract**. On a floured work area, roll out the dough and cut into 1½ inch circles. Bake at 350° for 10-12 minutes. When they are cool, spread half the circles with **1 teaspoon orange marmalade** and place another circle on top. Melt **1 cup chocolate** or **vanilla candy coating**. Dip half of each sandwich into the candy coating. Allow to cool on wax paper.

About 24g carbs per cookie sandwich

Pumpkin Spice Cookies

Use half of the basic dough. Add **2 teaspoons pumpkin pie spice**. Shape into 1 inch. Bake at 350° for 10-12 minutes. Frost with cream cheese frosting.

About 13g carbs per 1½ inch cookie

Spritz

Using half of the cookie dough, add ½ **teaspoon almond extract** and mix well. Color and shape, or use in a cookie press. Bake at 350° for 10-12 minutes.

About 7g carbs for a 1 inch cookie

Windowpane Cookies

Use half of the basic dough. Roll it out on a floured work surface. Use a cookie cutter with an identical one that is smaller. Cut out all the cookies with the larger shape, then cut holes in half of them with the smaller shape. Bake at 350° for 10-12 minutes. When cool, spread **jam** on the whole cookies and place the ones with holes on top.

About 26g carbs per 1½ inch sandwich

Double Chocolate Brownies

⅔ cup butter
5 ounces unsweetened chocolate, cut into pieces
1½ cups sugar
2 teaspoons vanilla
3 eggs
1 cup flour
½ teaspoon xanthan gum
1 cup chocolate chips

Preheat the oven to 350°. Grease a 9x9 inch square pan. In a microwave safe bowl, melt the butter. Add the unsweetened chocolate, and cook in 30 second increments just until melted. In a medium bowl, beat the sugar, vanilla, and eggs on high for 2-3 minutes.

Beat in the chocolate mixture on low speed. Add the flour and xanthan gum. Stir in the chocolate chips and spread into the prepared pan. Bake for 40 minutes or until the brownies start to pull away from the sides. Makes 16 brownies.

Total carbs 300g
About 13g carbs per 2 inch square
About 7g carbs per 1 inch brownie bites

Gingerbread for Houses

Gingerbread:
⅓ cup butter, softened
¼ cup sugar
¼ cup molasses
1 egg
2 cups flour
1 teaspoon cinnamon
1 teaspoon ginger

2 teaspoons xanthan gum
½ teaspoon baking powder
½ teaspoon salt

Frosting:
3 tablespoons meringue powder
4 cups powdered sugar
5 to 6 tablespoons warm water

Preheat the oven to 350° and grease several cookie sheets. Beat the butter, sugar, molasses, and egg until blended. Add the remaining ingredients in a separate bowl and mix until well blended. Roll out about ¼ inch thick on a floured surface, cut into house pieces, and bake ½ inch apart on the cookie sheets for 15 minutes or until no longer soft.

While they are still hot, trim the edges of the pieces so that the lines are straight. Cool on racks. In a medium bowl, mix the frosting ingredients. Place the frosting in a pastry bag or zipper bag with one corner cut off.

Glue the pieces together with the frosting on small pieces of cardboard covered with foil or salad plates. Glue on candy pieces with the frosting. Makes 3 small houses or 1 large house.

Total carbs 300g for the dough
Each house with frosting and candy
will need to be individually calculated

Roof of House
Cut two per house

Side of House
Cut two per house

Front of House
Cut two per house

Graham Crackers

1½ cups flour
¾ cup brown rice flour
½ cup brown sugar
1¾ teaspoons cinnamon
1½ teaspoons baking powder
¾ teaspoon xanthan gum

½ teaspoon salt
7 tablespoons butter, chilled

3-4 tablespoons cold water
3 tablespoons honey
1 teaspoon vanilla

Preheat the oven to 350° and grease several cookie sheets. In a large bowl, mix the dry ingredients, flour through salt, and cut the butter into the mixture. Add the water, honey, and vanilla and mix until it's a manageable dough, adding a little more water if necessary.

Refrigerate for 1 hour. Roll out dough ⅛ – ¼ inch thickness on a floured surface. Prick lightly with a fork and cut into squares. Place the squares ½ inch apart on the cookie sheets. Bake for 12-15 minutes. Cool several minutes on the cookie sheets before transferring to cooling racks.

Total carbs 370g

The thickness and size of the graham crackers will determine individual carb count
Make all of them the same size and then divide the total carbs
by how many graham crackers you have

Macaroons

⅓ cup butter, softened
3 ounces cream cheese, softened
¾ cup sugar
1 egg
1½ teaspoons almond extract
2 cups flour
2 teaspoons baking powder

½ teaspoon xanthan gum
½ teaspoon salt
3 cups flaked coconut

2 cups flaked coconut
48 chocolate kisses (optional)

In a large bowl, cream the butter, cream cheese, and sugar. Beat in the egg and almond extract. When fluffy, add in the flour, baking powder, xanthan gum, and salt and beat until well mixed. Add the 3 cups of the coconut and mix until well incorporated. Refrigerate for 1 hour.

Preheat the oven to 350°. Place the remaining 2 cups of coconut in a shallow bowl. Roll the dough into one inch balls and then roll each ball in the coconut until well coated. Place on ungreased cookie sheets and bake for 10-12 minutes.

If desired, press a chocolate kiss in the center of each cookie as soon as you take them out of the oven. Cool several minutes on the cookie sheets before transferring to cooling racks.

Total carbs 510g – without the chocolate kisses
About 8g carbs per cookie without the chocolate kisses
About 12g carbs per cookie with the chocolate kiss

Oatmeal Raisin Cookies

½ cup sugar
½ cup brown sugar
½ cup butter, softened
½ teaspoon baking soda
½ teaspoon cinnamon
½ teaspoon vanilla
½ teaspoon xanthan gum
¼ teaspoon baking powder

¼ teaspoon salt
1 egg

1½ cups GF oats
1¾ cups flour
1 cup raisins

Preheat the oven to 350° and grease several cookie sheets. In a large bowl, add all the ingredients except the oats, flour, and raisins. Mix well. Stir in the oats, flour, and raisins. Drop 1 inch spoonfuls of the dough onto cookie sheets about 2 inches apart. Bake about 9-10 minutes or until lightly browned. Cool several minutes on the cookie sheets before transferring to cooling racks.

Total carbs 625g
About 20g carbs per 1½ inch cookie

❖ Apple Cinnamon Oatmeal Cookies

Use 1 cup of cut up **dried apples** instead of the raisins and increase the **cinnamon** to 2 teaspoons.

Total carbs 625g
About 20g carbs per 1½ inch cookie

Peanut Butter Cookies

½ cup butter
¾ cup peanut butter
1¼ cups flour
½ cup sugar
½ cup brown sugar
1 egg
½ teaspoon baking soda
½ teaspoon baking powder
½ teaspoon xanthan gum

1 cup milk chocolate chips or M&Ms (optional)

Preheat the oven to 350° and grease several cookie sheets. Beat the butter and peanut butter until well blended. Add the remaining ingredients and beat until thoroughly combined. Add chocolate chips or M&Ms if desired. Shape into 1 inch balls and place on the cookie sheets. Flatten with a fork. Bake for 8-10 minutes or until lightly browned. Cool on the pan for several minutes before moving to a cooling rack.

Total carbs 370g - not including chocolate chips or M&Ms

Peanut Chocolate Candy Bars

Layer 1:
1 batch of chocolate chip cookie dough

Layer 2:
⅓ cup light corn syrup
3 tablespoons butter, softened
3 tablespoons peanut butter
1½ tablespoons water
1½ teaspoons vanilla
Dash of salt
3½ cups powdered sugar

Layer 3:
1 bag caramels, unwrapped
1 tablespoon water
1½ cups roasted peanuts

Layer 4:
2 cups chocolate chips

Preheat the oven to 350°. Line a 9x13 pan with foil and press the cookie dough evenly into the pan. Bake 18-20 minutes and then cool for 30 minutes. In a large bowl, mix the layer 2 ingredients until smooth and creamy. Filling will be thick. Press the filling over the cooled cookie crust.

In a microwavable bowl, melt the caramels with the 1 tablespoon of water, about 2 minutes on high. Stir in the nuts and spread over the filling. Refrigerate for 15 minutes.

Melt the chocolate chips in the microwave, 1-2 minutes on high. Spread over the caramel layer and refrigerate for 1 hour until the chocolate is set. Remove the bars using the foil and cut into 1 by 2 inch bars. Store in the fridge or freezer. Makes about 56 bars.

To make the bars more like candy bars, skip layer 4 and dip the cooled, cut up bars in melted chocolate candy coating.

Total carbs 1660g
About 30g carbs per bar

Raspberry Cheesecake Bars

Crust and Crumb Topping:
½ cup sugar
1½ cups flour
¾ teaspoon xanthan gum
1 teaspoon baking powder
1 teaspoon egg replacer
¼ teaspoon salt
½ cup butter

16 ounces cream cheese, softened
2 tablespoons sugar

1 teaspoon vanilla
1 egg

¾ cup raspberry jam
⅓ cup sliced almonds

Glaze:
½ cup powdered sugar
1-2 teaspoons water

Preheat the oven to 350°. Line a 9x13 cake pan with foil and grease it well. Mix the sugar through salt in a large bowl. Cut the butter into the mixture until it resembles coarse crumbs. Press ⅔ of the mixture into the pan, and set aside the remaining ⅓ for the topping. Bake for 10 minutes.

In a large bowl, beat the cream cheese, sugar, vanilla, and egg until smooth. Gently spread the cream cheese mixture over the crust. Spoon the jam over the cream cheese and then sprinkle the remaining crumbs over the jam. Top with the sliced almonds.

Bake for 35-40 minutes or until golden brown. Cool for 30 minutes and then place in fridge for 2 hours until completely cooled. Remove the bars from the pan using the foil. Mix the glaze ingredients in a small bowl and drizzle over the top and allow it to harden. Cut into 1½ inch squares. Store in the refrigerator or freezer. Makes about 35 squares.

Total carbs 560g
About 16g carbs per squares

Russian Tea Cakes

1 cup butter
¾ cup powdered sugar
½ teaspoon salt
1 teaspoon vanilla
2¾ cups flour
1½ teaspoons xanthan gum
1 cup pecans, finely chopped
Powdered sugar

Preheat the oven to 350°. In a large bowl, cream the butter and sugar. Add remaining ingredients and mix well. Form the dough into 1 inch balls. Place on an ungreased cookie sheet and bake for 10 minutes. Cool on the cookie sheet for several minutes before rolling in powdered sugar and place on a cooling rack. Cool completely and roll in powdered sugar again.

Total carbs 296g
About 10g carbs per cookie

Simple Microwave Fudge

4 cups chocolate chips
1 -14 ounce can sweetened condensed milk
3 tablespoons butter

Line a 9x13 pan with foil. In a microwave safe bowl, melt the butter in the microwave. Add the chocolate chips and melt using 30 second increments until just melted. Don't overcook. Add the condensed milk and mix until smooth and creamy. Mix in any additional ingredients that sound good to you. See below for suggestions.

Pour into the prepared pan and refrigerate for several hours, until set. Remove the fudge from the pan, using the foil. Cut into 1 inch squares. Place in an airtight container. Keep refrigerated, or freeze until you're ready to serve.

❖ Variations:

Pecan fudge: Add ½ cup finely chopped pecans
Berry fudge: Add ½ cup fresh blackberries or raspberries
Marshmallow fudge: Add ½ cup mini marshmallows
Toffee fudge: Add ½ cup toffee pieces

Total carbs 720g without any additions
About 15g carbs per 1 inch square

Snickerdoodles

½ cup butter
½ cup sugar
⅓ cup brown sugar
1 egg
½ teaspoon vanilla
1½ cups flour
1½ teaspoons xanthan gum
½ teaspoon baking soda
¼ teaspoon cream of tartar
¼ teaspoon salt

¼ cup cinnamon sugar

Preheat the oven to 350° and grease several cookie sheets. In a large bowl, cream the butter and sugars together, then add the egg and vanilla. Add the remaining ingredients except the cinnamon sugar, flour through salt. Beat until smooth. Roll the dough into 1 inch balls and coat the balls in cinnamon sugar. Place on the cookie sheet 1½ inches apart. Bake for 10-12 minutes. Cool on the pan for several minutes before moving to a cooling rack.

Total carbs 316g
About 15g carbs per 1½ inch cookie

Turtle Bars

Crust:
2 cups flour
¾ cup brown sugar
½ cup butter, softened
¼ teaspoon xanthan gum

1 cup pecan or walnut pieces

⅔ cup butter
½ cup brown sugar

1 cup chocolate chips

Preheat the oven to 350° and line a 9x13 pan with foil. In a medium bowl combine the crust ingredients, flour through xanthan gum. Once mixed, press evenly into the pan. Arrange the nuts over the crust.

In a small sauce pan, bring the butter and brown sugar to a boil. Cook for 3 minutes. Pour over the nuts and bake for 18-20 minutes.

Remove from the oven and sprinkle with the chocolate chips. Let the chocolate to melt for a few minutes before gently spreading the chocolate over the top, leaving some chips whole. Allow to cool completely before cutting into 1½ inch bars. Makes about 35 bars.

Total carbs 530g
About 15g carbs per bar

Notes:

_____

_____

_____

_____

_____

_____

_____

_____

_____

_____

_____

_____

_____

_____

_____

_____

_____

_____

_____

_____

_____

Desserts

Apricot Thyme Rustic Tart

Crust:
¼ cup flour
7 tablespoons water
⅛ teaspoon vinegar
⅛ teaspoon almond extract

1 cup flour
3 tablespoons sugar
¼ cup almond flour
½ teaspoon xanthan gum
¼ teaspoon salt
¼ cup cold butter

Filling:
2 tablespoons flour
2 tablespoons sugar
2 - 15 ounce cans apricots, drained

1 tablespoon honey
2 tablespoons sugar

1 teaspoon fresh thyme (optional)

Preheat the oven to 400° and grease a large cookie sheet. In a small bowl, mix the ¼ cup flour, water, vinegar, and almond extract to make a slurry. In another bowl, combine the 1 cup flour through salt and cut the butter into the mixture until coarse crumbs form. Add the slurry to the crumbs and kneed 5-10 times. Roll out the dough into a circle on a floured piece of plastic wrap. Use the plastic wrap to place the dough on the cookie sheet. Remove the plastic.

Sprinkle the 2 tablespoons flour and sugar on the dough. Arrange the drained apricots in spokes on top leaving a 2 inch boarder. Fold the border over the edges of the apricots. Spread the honey over the apricots and the crust edges. Sprinkle the remaining 2 tablespoons of sugar over the top. Bake for 35 minutes or until the crust browns. Remove from the oven and sprinkle with thyme.

Total carbs 346g
About 43g carbs per ⅛ serving

Apple Crisp

6 medium apples, chopped

½ cup butter
¾ cup brown sugar
1 cup flour
¾ cup almond meal
½ cup GF oats
¾ teaspoon cinnamon
¾ teaspoon nutmeg
Dash of salt

Heat the oven to 375°. Grease a square 9x9 pan. Arrange the apples in the pan. Mix the remaining ingredients in a medium bowl with a pastry cutter until completely blended and sticking together. Sprinkle over the apples. Bake for 30 minutes until the top is golden brown and the apples are tender.

Total carbs 400g

Baked Apples

2 cups dried cranberries
1 cup pecans, chopped
¾ cup brown sugar
1 cup water
1½ teaspoons cinnamon
½ teaspoon nutmeg
6 medium apples, chopped

Preheat the oven to 350° and grease a 9x9 baking dish. Combine all the ingredients. Place in the dish and bake for 30-35 minutes, stirring occasionally.

Total carbs 500g

Berry Mousse

2 cups fresh berries, or frozen berries, thawed
3 tablespoons sugar
2 ounces cream cheese, softened
2 cups whipped topping

Place the berries, sugar, and cream cheese in a blender and process until smooth. In a large bowl, gently combine the berry mixture with the whipped topping. Place in serving dishes and keep refrigerated until ready to serve.

Total carbs 110g
About 14g carbs per ½ cup serving

Blueberry-Cranberry Crumble Pie

½ recipe of pie crust (see page 154)

Crumb topping:
¾ cup flour
⅓ cup brown sugar
⅓ cup sugar
1 teaspoon cinnamon
⅛ teaspoon salt
½ cup butter

Filling:
3 cups blueberries
2 cups fresh cranberries
⅓ cup brown sugar
1 teaspoon cinnamon
¼ cup flour

1 tablespoon flour
1 tablespoon sugar

Preheat the oven to 350°. Roll out the pie crust and line a 9 inch pie plate. Bake the crust for 10 minutes. Make the crumb topping by mixing the flour through salt in a medium bowl, and cutting the butter into mixture until it forms coarse crumbs. Set aside.

In a large bowl, mix the berries with the brown sugar, cinnamon, and flour. Sprinkle the remaining flour and sugar into the bottom of the crust. Pour the berries over the top and sprinkle with the crumb topping. Bake for 50-60 minutes.

Total carbs 475g
About 60g carbs per ⅛ slice

Cherry Cheesecake Cobbler

8 ounces cream cheese, softened
⅓ cup sugar
⅓ cup flour
1 egg
1 teaspoon vanilla
½ teaspoon almond extract

¼ cup butter
¼ cup flour
4 cups frozen cherries, thawed
   (save the juice)
¼ cup sugar
¾ cup water

Gluten free sugar cookie crumbs (optional)

Heat the oven to 350° and grease a 1.5 quart casserole dish. In a medium bowl, beat the cream cheese and sugar until well blended. Add the ⅓ cup flour, egg, vanilla, and almond extract and mix well again. Set aside.

In a medium sauce pan, melt the butter, add the remaining ¼ cup flour and mix. Then add the cherries, cherry juice, sugar, and water. Cook until thick and bubbly.

Place the cherry mixture in the casserole dish. Spoon the cream cheese mixture over the cherries. Sprinkle the cookie crumbs over the top, and bake for 30-35 minutes. Cool slightly before serving.

Total carbs 266g

Chocolate Coconut Cream Pie

½ recipe of pie crust (see page 154)

A double recipe of vanilla pudding (see page 153)
½ cup flaked coconut

3 tablespoons unsweetened cocoa
3 tablespoons sugar
2 tablespoons milk

2 cups whipped cream

Preheat the oven to 350°. Line a 9 inch pie plate with the crust. Bake for 10 minutes. Meanwhile, make the vanilla pudding according to the directions. In a medium bowl, mix the flaked coconut and 2 cups of the vanilla pudding. Set aside.

Add the cocoa, sugar, and milk to the remaining 2 cups of pudding in the pan and heat until bubbly. Place 1 cup of the chocolate pudding to the bottom of the pie crust. Add half of the coconut pudding and then layer the remaining chocolate pudding and coconut pudding to make 4 layers total. Cool in the refrigerator.

Top with whipped cream before serving.

Total carbs- 440g
About 30g carbs per ⅛ slice without whipped cream

Fruit Pizza

Crust:
1 cup flour
⅓ cup powdered sugar
6 tablespoons butter, melted
1 teaspoon xanthan gum

Middle:
8 ounces cream cheese, softened
⅓ cup sugar
¼ teaspoon vanilla

Top:
2 cups fresh fruit

Preheat the oven to 350°. Using a pastry cutter, mix the crust ingredients in a medium bowl, until crumbs form. Dump the dough onto an ungreased, 12 inch pizza pan. Press the dough out to fill the pan. Bake for 10-15 minutes. Cool completely.

In a medium bowl, beat the cream cheese until smooth. Add the sugar and vanilla. Spread over the cooled crust. Top with your favorite fresh fruit.

Total carbs without fruit 200g
Add carbs for the fruit

Mexican Rice Pudding

½ cup uncooked rice
1½ cups water
1 small piece of lemon peel

3 cups milk
¼ cup sugar
¼ teaspoon salt
1½ teaspoons vanilla
1 cinnamon stick

Cinnamon sugar

In a large pot, cook the rice in the water with the lemon peel and cinnamon stick until done, about 15-18 minutes. Mix in the milk, sugar, salt, vanilla, and cinnamon stick. Simmer uncovered until thick and the rice has absorbed most of the milk, stirring frequently to prevent burning. Serve warm sprinkled with cinnamon sugar.

This can also be placed in a blender for smoother pudding

Total carbs 190g
About 22g carbs per ½ cup serving

Norwegian Fruit Soup

5½ cups water
¼ cup pearl tapioca
½ cup raisins
½ cup prunes
½ cup dried apricots
⅔ cup sugar
1 small lemon, sliced
1 stick cinnamon
1 cup grape juice

In a large pot, add all the ingredients except the grape juice. Simmer for 1½ hours stirring frequently. Add the grape juice and cook a little longer. Serve warm or cold by itself, or over vanilla ice cream.

Total carbs 318g – without the ice cream
About 20g carbs per ½ cup serving

Pecan Pie

½ recipe of pie crust (see page 154)

3 large eggs
¾ cup sugar
⅔ cup light corn syrup
2 tablespoons butter, melted
2 teaspoons vanilla
¼ teaspoon salt
2 cups pecan halves

Preheat the oven to 350°. Line a 9 inch pie plate with the crust. In a medium bowl, mix the remaining ingredients and pour into the pie crust. Bake for 55-60 minutes or until set. Serve warm or cold.

Total carbs 490g
About 61g carbs per ⅛ slice

Rhubarb, Berry Cobbler

Filling:
1½ cups rhubarb, chopped
½ cup blueberries
1 cup strawberries
1 tablespoon lemon juice
1 teaspoon vanilla
Dash of nutmeg

Streusel Topping:
5 tablespoons cold butter
⅔ cup flour
⅓ cup almond meal
¼ cup sugar
½ teaspoon cinnamon

Heat the oven to 350° and grease a 9x9 pan. In a medium bowl, mix all the filling ingredients and place in the pan. In a smaller bowl, use a pastry cutter to mix the streusel ingredients until coarse crumbs form. Sprinkle evenly on top of the fruit and bake for 30-35 minutes.

Total carbs 200g
About 34g carbs per ½ cup serving

Rhubarb Pie

1 recipe of pie crust (see page 154)

4 cups fresh rhubarb, chopped
1½ cups sugar
A pinch of salt
¼ cup flour
2 teaspoons tapioca

1 egg
2 teaspoons water

1 tablespoon butter

Preheat the oven to 350° and make 1 batch of pie crust. Line a 9 inch pie plate with half of the pie crust. In a large bowl, combine the rhubarb, sugar, salt, flour, and tapioca. In a small bowl, mix the egg and water and then add it to the rhubarb.

Place the rhubarb mixture in the pie plate and dot with butter. Cover with the remaining pastry, seal the edges, and cut slits in the top. Bake for 40-45 minutes or until crust is golden brown and filling is bubbling.

Total carbs 530g
About 66g carbs per ⅛ piece

Rømmegrøt

(Norwegian cream pudding)

½ cup butter
¾ cup flour
4 cups milk
1 cup cream
½ cup sugar

Melted butter and cinnamon sugar

In a large pot, melt the butter. Add the flour and mix until smooth. Add the milk and cream. Cook until thick and bubbly, stirring constantly. Add the sugar. Serve with melted butter and cinnamon sugar on top.

Total carbs 170g
About 25g carbs per ½ cup serving with cinnamon sugar on top.

S'mores Dip

(For when you can't have a fire, but you have the craving)

1 cup chocolate chips
2 tablespoons milk
1½ cups mini-marshmallows - divided

GF graham crackers

Turn oven on to broil. In a microwave safe bowl, melt the chocolate chips, milk, and 1 cup of the marshmallows in 30 second increments until melted. Pour into a 9 inch pie plate.

Top with the remaining ½ cup of marshmallows. Place the pie plate under the broiler for one minute or until the marshmallows are slightly browned. Serve with the graham crackers for dipping.

Total carbs 160g - without the graham crackers

Vanilla Pudding

⅓ cup sugar
2 tablespoons flour
Pinch of salt
2 cups milk
2 egg yolks
2 tablespoons butter
1½ teaspoons vanilla

Mix the sugar, cornstarch, salt, and milk in a medium sauce pan over medium heat. Cook until thick and bubbly, stirring frequently. Whisk the egg yolks in a small bowl. Whisk half of the hot mixture into the egg yolks stirring vigorously. Gradually add the egg mixture back into the pan, still stirring well. Cook 1 minute longer, stirring constantly. Remove from heat and add the butter and vanilla. Stir until the butter is melted and mixed in.

Total carbs 100g – About 25g carbs per ½ cup serving

Variations:

❖ **Chocolate Pudding**
Increase the sugar to ½ cup and add ⅓ cup cocoa powder with the milk.

Total carbs 135g – About 34g carbs per ½ cup serving

❖ **Butterscotch Pudding**
Use ½ cup brown sugar instead of white sugar.

Total carbs 135g – About 34g carbs per ½ cup serving

-Crusts-

Basic Pie Crust

2¼ cups flour
2 teaspoons xanthan gum
¼ teaspoon salt
¼ teaspoon vanilla
¾ cup butter (do not substitute)
⅓ to ½ cup very cold water

In a large bowl, mix the flour, xanthan gum, and salt. Add the butter and vanilla and using a pastry cutter, cut until the crumbs are pea sized. Add the water a bit at a time until you can form the dough into two balls. Spread several sheets of plastic wrap on the counter to form a large work area. Sprinkle the plastic wrap well with flour. Roll out one ball on the plastic wrap. You may need to sprinkle a little flour on top to keep the rolling pin from sticking.

Using the plastic wrap, gently flip the rolled out dough into a pie plate and remove the plastic. Fill the pie with your favorite filling. Roll out the second ball of dough on the plastic wrap and gently flip it on top of the filling. Seal the edges and bake according to the filling directions, or freeze extra dough.

Total carbs 225g
About 200g when used for a pie (minus scraps) - 100g for a single crust
About 25g carbs per ⅛ piece of double crusted pie without filling
About 13g carbs for ⅛ piece of single crusted pie without filling

Nut Crust

1½ cups toasted pecans, almonds or walnuts, ground in a blender
2 tablespoons butter, softened
3 tablespoons brown sugar

In a medium bowl mix all the ingredients with a pastry cutter until coarse crumbs form. Press into a pie plate or springform pan. Bake at 350° for 10 minutes. Fill with your desired filling.

Total carbs 45g for the nut crust

Streusel Topping

5 tablespoons cold butter
⅔ cup flour
⅓ cup almond meal
¼ cup sugar
½ teaspoon cinnamon

In a medium bowl, cut the butter into the flour until it forms coarse crumbs. Mix in the remaining ingredients and sprinkle on top of muffins, cobblers or cakes.

Total carbs 132g

Notes:

Beef Recipes

❖

Any recipe with an * is one that can be made in about 30 minutes

Basic Meatloaf

½ cup onion, chopped
1 clove garlic, minced
¼ cup ketchup
¼ cup milk
1 tablespoon mustard
1 teaspoon salt
½ teaspoon pepper
1 egg
1 slice GF bread, crumbled
1 pound ground beef

Ketchup or barbeque sauce

Preheat the oven to 350° and grease a 9x9 pan. Mix all ingredients except the ground beef in a medium bowl, onion through bread. Add the ground beef and mix well. Pour the meat into the pan and form into a loaf. Squirt ketchup or barbeque sauce over the top. Bake for 35-40 minutes.

Total carbs 48g
About 6g carbs per slice

Baked Beef Stew

2 pounds beef, cubed
2 medium onions, thinly sliced

1½ cups beef broth
½ cup red wine
¼ cup red wine vinegar
1 teaspoon thyme
1 teaspoon rosemary
1 teaspoon salt
½ teaspoon pepper

2 tablespoons flour
3 cups baby carrots

Preheat oven to 450° and grease a 3 quart casserole dish. Place the beef in the dish along with the onions. Bake uncovered for 50 minutes, stirring occasionally. While the meat is cooking, combine the broth, wine, vinegar, thyme, rosemary, salt and pepper.

Remove the beef from the oven and reduce oven temperature to 350°. Sprinkle the beef with flour and stir gently to coat. Pour the broth mixture over the meat and stir to loosen any browned bits. Add the carrots, cover the dish with foil, and bake for 2 - 2½ hours more.

Total carbs 50g
About 7g carbs per 1 cup serving

Beef Stroganoff *

2 tablespoons olive oil
1½ cups onion, thinly sliced
1 cup mushrooms, sliced
1½ pounds steak, thinly sliced
2 tablespoons flour
1 teaspoon salt
½ teaspoon pepper

1 – 8 ounce can tomato sauce
1½ tablespoon Worcestershire sauce
½ cup white wine

½ cup sour cream

Hot cooked GF noodles

Heat the oil over medium heat in a large frying pan. Add the onions and mushrooms and cook until tender, about 5 minutes. Remove them from the pan and keep warm. Add the steak to the pan and cook in batches just until it's done.

Return all the meat, mushrooms and onions to the pan. Sprinkle the meat with the flour, salt, and pepper and mix well. Add the tomato sauce, Worcestershire sauce, and white wine. Cook one minute longer until it's heated through and the sauce has thickened. Remove from heat and add the sour cream. Serve over hot cooked noodles.

Total carbs 40g, not including noodles

Beef Tenderloin with Balsamic Sauce *

4 beef tenderloin steaks (about 2 pounds)
2 teaspoons salt
1 teaspoon pepper
2 tablespoons olive oil

Sauce:
½ cup red wine
3 tablespoons balsamic vinegar
1 green onion, finely chopped
2 cloves garlic, minced
2 teaspoons flour
⅓ cup butter, melted

Preheat the oven to 350°. Rub the steaks with salt and pepper. Barbeque the meat until desired doneness, or in a large, oven-proof frying pan, seer the steaks on both sides in hot olive oil (about 2-3 minutes). Place the frying pan in the oven, flipping once, for 8-15 minutes depending on the desired doneness.

While the steaks are cooking, whisk the first 5 ingredients of the sauce together in a medium sauce pan, wine through flour. Cook over medium heat until thick. Add the butter and whisk until blended. Serve the sauce over the steaks.

Total carbs 12g from the sauce only
About 1½g carbs per tablespoon of sauce

Bolognese Pasta Sauce

2 tablespoons olive oil
1 carrot, finely chopped
1 stalk celery, finely chopped
½ cup onion, finely chopped
¼ cup mushrooms, sliced

½ pound ground beef
¼ pound Italian sausage
¼ cup white wine
1 cup water

3 tomatoes, chopped
1 tablespoon fresh parsley
¼ teaspoon nutmeg
1 teaspoon salt
½ teaspoon pepper

Hot cooked GF noodles
Parmesan cheese

In a large frying pan, cook the veggies over medium heat in the olive oil until they are almost burnt, 10-15 minutes. Add the ground beef and sausage, and cook until the meat is done. Add the wine and cook until it's almost evaporated. Stir in the remaining ingredients, except the noodles and parmesan cheese and simmer for one hour.

Serve over noodles and garnish with parmesan cheese.

Total carbs 15g - not including noodles

Bursa Kabobs

(Turkish cuisine)

2 pounds steak
1 onion, thinly sliced
2 cloves garlic, minced
1 green bell pepper, thinly sliced
⅓ cup olive oil
¼ cup fresh parsley, chopped
2 tablespoons fresh oregano, chopped

2 bay leaves
1 teaspoon fresh thyme, chopped
1 teaspoon salt
½ teaspoon pepper
1 cup white wine

Mix all the ingredients and place in a shallow dish with the meat to marinate overnight.

Make the Mediterranean Cucumber Salad (see page 331), the Pita Bread (see page 25) and the Turkish Tomato Sauce (see page 343).

Preheat the oven to broil. Place the meat and marinade along with the peppers and onions on a foil-lined cookie sheet with edges, and broil until desired doneness, flipping once, about 8-10 minutes. When the meat reaches desired doneness, slice it thin and serve with the onions and peppers over ripped up pita bread with the Turkish tomato sauce and Mediterranean cucumber salad.

Total carbs – Meat and marinade – 15g carbs
Turkish Tomato Sauce – 60g carbs (about 8g carbs per ½ cup)
Cucumber salad – 18g carbs (about 5g carbs per ½ cup)
Flat bread (about 27g carbs per piece of flat bread)

Cincinnati Chili *

2 teaspoons oil
1½ pounds lean ground beef
⅓ cup onion, chopped
3 tablespoons chili powder
¾ teaspoon ground cinnamon
¾ teaspoon ground cumin
⅛ teaspoon ground allspice
⅛ teaspoon ground cloves
⅛ teaspoon cayenne pepper
1 bay leaf
1 tablespoon vinegar
1 - 8 ounce can tomato sauce

Hot cooked GF spaghetti noodles
Grated cheddar cheese

In a large sauce pan, brown the beef in the oil. Add the onions and cook until the onions are tender. Add the remaining ingredients and allow to simmer for 15-20 minutes. Serve the meat sauce over the noodles and top with cheese.

Total carbs 15g - not including the noodles

Cheeseburger Salad *

5-6 GF bread crusts, lightly buttered
1½ pounds ground beef
1 small red onion - ½ diced, ½ thinly sliced
½ cup dill pickles, diced
½ cup ketchup
1 tablespoon mustard
8-10 cups lettuce, sliced
1 cup cheddar cheese, grated
2 tomatoes, chopped

Preheat the oven to 425°. Cut the buttered bread crusts into strips and arrange on a large baking sheet. Bake 8-10 minutes or until lightly toasted. Remove and cool.

Cook the ground beef in a large skillet until no longer pink. In a large bowl combine the onion, pickles, ketchup, and mustard. Add the cooked beef and mix well.

Place the lettuce on plates. Spoon the beef mixture over the lettuce and top with cheese, tomatoes and sliced onion. Serve the "bun" croutons on the side.

Total carbs 20g - plus carbs from the bread crusts

Deep Dish Pizza

1 batch of Basic White Bread (see page 14)

1 tablespoon oil
1 pound ground beef
1 teaspoon salt
⅓ cup onion, chopped
2 cloves garlic, minced

1 - 16 ounce can crushed tomatoes
1 tablespoon Italian seasonings

½ red bell pepper, chopped
¼ cup sliced mushrooms
Pepperoni slices
1½ cups shredded mozzarella cheese

Make the bread dough. Using well-floured hands, line the bottom and sides of a greased 9x13 pan with the dough. Place in a warm place to rise for 30 minutes.

Preheat the oven to 400°. In a large frying pan, brown the ground beef in the oil. Add the salt, onion, and garlic and cook until soft. Spread the beef over the crust once it's risen. Mix the Italian seasonings into the tomatoes and spread over the meat. Top with the bell peppers, mushrooms, pepperoni, and cheese.

Bake for 20-25 minutes. If cheese starts to brown, cover with foil. Cut into 10 squares and serve.

Total carbs 390g
About 39g carbs per square

Fajitas

1 batch of GF flour tortillas (see page 21)

Marinade:
⅓ cup lime juice
3 tablespoons olive oil
1 tablespoon GF soy sauce
4 cloves garlic, minced
1 teaspoon salt
½ teaspoon cayenne pepper
¼ teaspoon black pepper
2 pounds steak (or boneless chicken)

Onions and Peppers:
1 tablespoon olive oil
1 large onion, thinly sliced
1 red bell pepper, thinly sliced
½ teaspoon salt
¼ teaspoon pepper
1 tablespoon lemon juice

Other Toppings:
Salsa, Sour cream, Guacamole, Shredded cheese

Mix together all the marinade ingredients in a medium bowl, including the meat cut into thin strips. Allow to marinate for at least 1 hour. Broil or pan fry the meat until it is cooked through.

In a medium frying pan, heat the remaining 1 tablespoon of olive oil over medium heat and add the onion and bell pepper. Sprinkle with salt and pepper and add the lemon juice. Cook until slightly browned. Serve the meat and onions and peppers on the flour tortillas with the other toppings of your choice.

Total carbs – Meat – 0g carbs
Onions and Peppers – 10g carbs
Tortillas – 217g carbs (About 22g carbs per tortilla)
Don't forget to include the carbs from other toppings you might add

Festive Taco Lasagna

1 pound ground beef
¼ cup onion, chopped
1 clove garlic, minced
2 teaspoons fresh chives, chopped
1 package taco seasoning
2 cups corn
½ cup water
4 ounces cream cheese
4½ cups salsa

6 cups tortilla chips, slightly crushed
2 cups shredded cheddar cheese

Sour cream
Guacamole

Preheat the oven to 350° and grease a 9x13 pan. In a large sauce pan, brown the ground beef. Add the onions, garlic, and chives and cook until they are soft. Add the taco seasoning, corn, water, cream cheese, and salsa.

Spread one cup of the sauce over the bottom of the pan. Build the first layer by place 1½ cups of tortilla chips over the sauce. Cover with another cup of sauce and a layer of cheddar cheese. Repeat the chips, sauce, and cheese for the next layers until you have three layers total. Bake for 30 minutes. Garnish with sour cream and guacamole.

Total carbs 300g carbs - without the sour cream and guacamole

French Dip Sandwiches

(This makes really nice roast beef as well)

2 pound roast
3 cups water
1½ cups beef broth
½ cup GF soy sauce
2 tablespoons Worcestershire sauce
2 cloves garlic, minced
1 teaspoon rosemary
2 bay leaves

GF buns (see page 15)

Cut the roast into 1½ inch slices. Place all the ingredients in a crock pot on low for 6-8 hours. Remove the beef and shred. Serve on buns with the remaining liquid for dipping.

Total carbs 0g - not including buns

Ham and Cheese Meat Roll

1 egg
1 slice of bread, crumbled
1 - 8 ounce can tomato sauce
1 tablespoon parsley, chopped
2 teaspoons oregano, chopped
2 cloves garlic, minced
1 teaspoon salt

½ teaspoon pepper
1 pound lean ground beef

6 thin slices of ham
1½ cups shredded mozzarella cheese - divided

Preheat the oven to 400° and grease a 9x9 pan. In a large bowl, beat the egg slightly and then add the next 7 ingredients, bread through pepper. Mix well and add in the ground beef. Spread the meat out on a piece of plastic wrap and pat it into an 8x10 inch rectangle. Lay the slices of ham on top of the meat and cover with 1 cup of the mozzarella cheese.

Starting at the short side, use the plastic wrap to help you roll the meat into a log and then to lift the roll seam-side down into the prepared pan. Bake for 40-45 minutes. Cover the top of the roll with the remaining mozzarella cheese and return it to the oven for a few more minutes, until the cheese melts.

Total carbs 35g

Home-Style Beef and Noodles *

1 tablespoon olive oil
1 pound steak, cut into chunks
½ cup celery, chopped
¼ cup onion, chopped
2 carrots, thinly sliced
2 cloves garlic, minced

3 cups beef broth
1 tablespoon flour

1 teaspoon salt
1 teaspoon Italian seasonings
½ teaspoon pepper
1 tablespoon balsamic vinegar

Hot cooked GF noodles

Place the oil in a large frying pan. Add the meat and cook until half done. Add the celery, onion, carrots, and garlic and keep cooking until the meat is done and the veggies are tender.

In a medium bowl, mix the beef broth and flour well, and add to the pan along with the remaining ingredients. Simmer for 15 minutes. Serve over hot noodles.

Total carbs 10g - not including noodles

Inner Mongolian Stir Fry *

(Outer Mongolia is its own country. Inner Mongolia is part of China)

1½ pounds steak, sliced thin
2 tablespoons oil
1 teaspoon garlic, minced
½ cup GF soy sauce
¼ cup sugar
2 teaspoons rice wine
3 cups snow peas, halved
1 teaspoon sesame oil

Hot cooked rice

Heat the oil in a large sauce pan or wok. Add the beef in small batches and cook until browned. Remove the cooked beef and keep warm. Add the garlic to the last batch of meat.

Mix the soy sauce, sugar, and wine. Add it to the pan along with the rest of the cooked beef and cook until the liquid is reduced by half. Add the snow peas and cook for 2 minutes longer. Add the sesame oil. Serve over hot cooked rice.

Total carbs 60g - not including rice

Italian Spiced Meatballs

Meatballs:
2 pounds ground beef
½ cup onion, minced
1 slice of bread, crumbled
2 cloves garlic, minced
1 egg
1 tablespoon parsley, chopped
2 teaspoons oregano, chopped
2 teaspoons basil, chopped
1 tablespoon olive oil
1 teaspoon salt
½ teaspoon pepper
¼ cup parmesan cheese

Topping:
¼ cup parmesan cheese
¼ teaspoon pepper
⅓ cup ricotta cheese

Tomato Sauce:
1 tablespoon olive oil
¼ cup onion, chopped
1 clove garlic, minced
1 – 8 ounce can tomato sauce
1 tablespoon Italian seasonings
½ teaspoon salt
1 teaspoon sugar
(Or use 1 cup prepared marinara sauce)

Preheat the oven to 400° and grease a 9x9 pan. In a large bowl, mix the ground beef with the remaining meatball ingredients. Shape into nine very large balls – about ½ cup of meat for each one. Place in the prepared pan and bake for about 40 minutes. In the meantime, mix the topping ingredients in a small bowl and set aside. In a small sauce pan, make the tomato sauce by cooking the onion and garlic in the olive oil until tender. Add the tomatoes, Italian seasonings, salt, and sugar and cook until heated through.

Remove the meatballs from the oven and turn the oven up to broil. Spoon a little of the cheese topping onto each meatball. Return them to the oven and broil for about 3 minutes or until the cheese is browned. Serve with the tomato sauce poured over the meatballs.

Total carbs 90g
About 10g carbs for one meat ball with sauce

Korean Marinated Beef

(Chicken also works really well)

¾ cup onion, finely chopped
1 clove garlic, minced
½ cup GF soy sauce
⅓ cup oil
2 tablespoons sugar
1 tablespoon sesame seeds
¼ teaspoon pepper
1½ pounds steak

Mix all ingredients except the steak in a shallow dish. Add the steak and marinate for at least 8 hours. Overnight is best. Barbeque or broil steak to desired doneness. The steak can also be sliced thin and marinated for several hours, then threaded on skewers or, cubed and alternated with veggies on skewers.

Total carbs 0g - not including skewer veggies

London Broil with Onions

2 pounds London broil steak

Marinade:
1½ cups onion, thinly sliced
2 cloves garlic, minced
⅓ cup lemon juice
2 tablespoons GF soy sauce

2 tablespoons olive oil
2 teaspoons sugar
1 teaspoon Italian seasonings
1 teaspoon lemon zest
1 teaspoon salt
¼ teaspoon pepper

Score the steak diagonally, about ⅛ inch deep. Place the steak in a large zippered plastic bag or large container with a lid. Mix marinade ingredients and add to steak, coating well. Marinate at least 2 hours or overnight.

Remove the steak from the marinade and barbeque until desired doneness or broil about 4 inches from heat, turning once. Meanwhile, place the onions and marinade in a large sauce pan and cook over high heat until the liquid has evaporated and the onions are slightly browned. Serve the steak with the onions on top.

Total carbs 20g - with onions

Manicotti

Meat Sauce:
1 pound ground beef
½ cup onion, chopped
½ cup mushrooms, sliced
2 cloves garlic, minced
½ cup black olives, sliced
1 - 24 ounce jar spaghetti sauce
1 - 8 ounce can tomato sauce

Cheese sauce:
3 tablespoons butter
3 tablespoons flour
2 cups milk
½ teaspoon salt
¼ teaspoon pepper
½ cup parmesan cheese

1 package GF jumbo shells

Preheat the oven to 350° and grease a 9x13 pan. Prepare the noodles according to package directions. In a medium sauce pan, brown the beef until done. Add the onion, mushrooms, and garlic and cook until tender. Add the black olives, spaghetti sauce and tomato sauce and set aside.

In another medium sauce pan, melt the butter. Add the flour and mix well. Add the milk and cook over medium-high heat, stirring frequently until it's thick. Add the salt, pepper, and parmesan cheese and mix well.

Place the cooked, drained noodles in the pan and fill with the meat sauce. Spoon the cheese sauce over the top and cover with foil. Bake for 30 minutes or until hot and bubbly.

Total carbs for the meat sauce 15g
Plus carbs from the jar of spaghetti sauce
Total carbs for the cheese sauce 36g carbs
Noodles – see package

Mediterranean Beef Pitas

Marinade:
2 teaspoons olive oil
1 tablespoon fresh rosemary, chopped
2 cloves garlic
½ teaspoon salt
¼ teaspoon pepper
1½ pounds steak, thinly sliced

Cucumber salad:
1 large cucumber, seeded and chopped
1 tablespoon lemon juice
⅛ teaspoon pepper
½ cup plain yogurt

1 recipe Pita bread (see page 25)
Sliced tomatoes

In a medium bowl, mix the oil through beef and let stand for 1 hour. Make the pita bread and cucumber salad while it marinates. Sauté the meat in a medium frying pan for 4-5 minutes or until browned.

For the salad combine the cucumber, lemon juice, pepper, and yogurt. Serve the meat, tomatoes, and cucumber salad inside the pitas.

Total carbs Meat 12g - not including Pitas

Mongolian Bohdz

(Authentic Mongolian meat dumplings. An acquired taste, but yummy if you've grown up with them. Kaia, Ross and Isaac, this one's for you)

Dough:
4 cups flour
2 teaspoons xanthan gum
2 teaspoons baking powder
2 tablespoons yeast
2 tablespoons sugar
½ teaspoon salt
1 cup warm water
1 tablespoon oil
1 egg

Filling:
1 pound ground beef
1 tablespoon oil
½ cup onion, chopped
1 clove garlic
1 teaspoon salt
½ teaspoon pepper

Kneed together all dough ingredients and set aside. In a large pan, cook the ground beef in the oil. When almost done, add the onion and garlic and cook until the veggies are tender.

Using 1 inch balls, roll the dough into very thin, flat circles. Place a spoonful of filling in the middle and pinch into a dumpling. Steam the dumplings in a shallow frying pan with a vegetable steamer over 1 inch of boiling water. Keep covered until the dumplings are cooked through, about 20 minutes. Serve with ketchup.

Total carbs 465g

Moroccan Beef or lamb Patties *

Patties:

1 egg

⅓ cup onion, finely chopped

⅓ cup milk

¼ cup soft bread crumbs

¼ cup fresh parsley, chopped

½ teaspoon salt

½ teaspoon ground cumin

¼ teaspoon coriander

¼ teaspoon cayenne pepper

1½ pounds ground beef *or* lamb

Yogurt Sauce:

½ cup plain yogurt

2 tablespoons fresh mint, chopped

¼ teaspoon sugar

In a medium bowl mix the patty ingredients. Add the ground beef or lamb and mix thoroughly. Form into patties and fry in a large, greased skillet until done. While the patties are cooking, mix all the yogurt sauce ingredients in a small bowl. Serve with a spoonful of yogurt sauce on each patty.

Total carbs meat patties 18g
Yogurt sauce 6g

Pepper Steak *

1 tablespoon oil
1 pound steak, thinly sliced
1 teaspoon salt
1 teaspoon pepper
1 bell pepper, chopped
½ cup onion, chopped
2 cloves garlic, minced
1 - 16 ounce can diced tomatoes
1 tablespoon Worcestershire sauce

Hot cooked rice

In a large frying pan, brown the steak in the oil. Sprinkle with salt and pepper while cooking. Add the bell pepper, onion, and garlic and cook until tender. Stir in the tomatoes and Worcestershire sauce and heat through. Serve over hot cooked rice.

Total carbs 35g – not including rice

Pizza in a Bowl *

4 ounces uncooked GF noodles
1 pound ground beef *or* ½ pound ground Italian sausage
½ cup pepperoni, diced
¼ cup mushrooms, sliced
½ cup green bell pepper, chopped
¼ cup onion, finely chopped
2 cloves garlic, minced
1 - 15 ounce can crushed tomato
1 tablespoon Italian seasonings
½ teaspoon salt

2 cups mozzarella cheese

Cook the noodles according to the package directions. Brown the sausage or beef in a large skillet. Add the pepperoni, mushrooms, bell pepper, onion, and garlic. Cook until veggies are tender. Add the tomatoes, Italian seasonings, and salt and heat through. Toss with the cooked, drained noodles. Sprinkle mozzarella cheese over the top, mix a little, and serve.

Total carbs 125g - including noodles

Polynesian Meatballs *

Meatballs:
⅓ cup onion, chopped
1 slice of GF bread, crumbled
1 teaspoon salt
¼ cup milk
1 egg
1½ pounds lean ground beef

1 tablespoon oil

Sauce:
1 – 20 ounce can of pineapple tidbits,
    undrained
2 tablespoons cornstarch
2 tablespoons vinegar
2 tablespoons GF soy sauce
2 tablespoons lemon juice
¼ cup brown sugar

Hot cooked rice

Combine the meatball ingredients in a medium bowl and mix well. Form into 1½ inch balls. In a large frying pan, cook them in the oil, turning at least once.

While they're cooking, mix the sauce ingredients in a medium bowl. When the meatballs are cooked through, add the sauce to the pan. Stir and cook until it's thick and bubbly. Serve over rice.

Total carbs 160g - not including rice

Quick Nachos *

1½ pounds ground beef (or shredded cooked chicken)
2 cloves garlic
6 green onions, diced - separate white and green parts.
1 cup salsa
2 tablespoons chili powder
½ teaspoon cumin
½ teaspoon oregano
1 teaspoon salt
½ teaspoon pepper

10-13 ounces tortilla chips
2 cups shredded cheddar cheese
1 tomato, chopped

Preheat the oven to 350° and line a large pizza pan with foil. In a large skillet, brown the ground beef, adding the garlic and white part of the onions at the very end. Cook for 1 minute more. Stir in the salsa and spices and cook until heated through.

Arrange the tortilla chips on the pan. Spoon the beef mixture over the chips. Spread the cheese and tomato over them. Bake for 10 minutes or until cheese has melted. Top with the green part of the onions before serving.

Total carbs Meat - 0g
Toppings - 35g
Chips per package

Salisbury Steak *

Patties:
¼ cup milk
⅓ cup bread crumbs
⅓ cup onion, chopped
2 teaspoons parsley
1½ pounds ground beef

2 tablespoons olive oil

Gravy:
1½ tablespoons butter
1½ tablespoons flour
1½ cups beef broth
5 tablespoons ketchup
1 teaspoon salt
½ teaspoon pepper

Hot cooked GF noodles

Mix the patty ingredients together in a medium bowl. Form into patties. Spread the olive oil in a large frying pan. Cook the patties over medium-high heat until done, turning at least once. Remove and keep warm in a serving dish. Melt the butter in the pan, add the flour and mix well. Add the broth and whisk until smooth. Cook until thick and bubbly. Then add the ketchup, salt, and pepper. Pour the gravy over the patties and serve with noodles.

Total carbs 50g – not including the noodles

Sauerbraten Pot Roast

½ cup ketchup
½ cup water
1 tablespoon sugar
2 tablespoons vinegar
1 tablespoon Worcestershire sauce
1 tablespoon prepared mustard
½ teaspoon salt
½ teaspoon allspice
¼ teaspoon pepper

¾ cup onion, chopped
1 bay leaf
1½ - 2 pound roast

1 cup water

1 tablespoon molasses
2 tablespoons flour
2 tablespoons water
½ teaspoon ginger

In a large container with a lid, mix the first 11 ingredients, ketchup through bay leaf. Cut the roast into 1 inch thick slices. Add the roast and marinate 6 hours or overnight. Place the meat and the marinade along with the remaining 1 cup of water in a crock pot.

Cook on high for 3-4 hours. Just before serving, remove the meat and keep warm. In a small bowl, mix the molasses, cornstarch, water and ginger. Add to the cooking liquid from the meat and cook in a medium pan over medium-high heat on the stove until it thickens. Serve over the meat.

Total carbs 80g

Shepherd's Pie

(Great for using up leftover beef, mashed potatoes, and veggies)

1 pound ground beef (or leftover roast beef)
½ cup onion, chopped
1 clove garlic, minced

½ cup ketchup
½ cup corn
½ cup peas (or leftover veggies)
2 teaspoons Worcestershire sauce
1 teaspoon salt
½ teaspoon pepper

3 cups mashed potatoes (or leftover mashed potatoes)
1 cup shredded cheddar cheese

Preheat the oven to 350° and grease a 9x13 pan. In a medium frying pan, brown the ground beef adding in the onions and garlic at the end. Cook until they're soft. Add the remaining ingredients except the mashed potatoes and cheese. Mix well and pour into the prepared pan. Top with the mashed potatoes and sprinkle the cheese on top. Cover with foil and bake for 30-35 minutes.

Total carbs 165g

Sloppy Joes *

1 tablespoon oil
1¼ pounds ground beef
½ cup onion, chopped
½ cup green bell pepper, chopped
1 clove garlic, minced

¼ cup brown sugar
1 – 8 ounce can tomato sauce
1 tablespoon Worcestershire sauce
1 tablespoon prepared mustard
1 teaspoon salt
½ teaspoon pepper
Tabasco sauce to taste

In a medium sauce pan, brown the meat in the oil. When it's almost brown, add the onion, bell pepper, and garlic and cook until veggies are soft. Add the remaining ingredients and cook until it's heated through. Serve on buns. (See page 15).

Total carbs 85g - not including the buns

Southwest Meatloaf

Meatloaf:
1½ pounds ground beef
1 cup onion, chopped
½ cup celery, chopped
½ cup red bell pepper, chopped
2 cloves garlic, minced
1 jalapeño pepper, chopped
1½ teaspoons cumin
3 tablespoons barbeque sauce
¾ cup oats
1 egg

⅓ cup ketchup
1 tablespoon mustard
1 teaspoon salt
½ teaspoon pepper
1 - 15 ounce can black beans,
    drained, rinsed and mashed

Toppings:
¼ cup barbeque sauce
¾ cup shredded cheddar cheese

Preheat the oven to 350° and grease a 9x13 pan. Mix all the meatloaf ingredients in a large bowl. Pour into the prepared pan and shape into a loaf. Bake for 40 minutes.

Top with remaining barbeque sauce and cheese and bake for 10 minutes longer. Let stand 5-10 minutes before slicing.

Total carbs 170g

Spaghetti *

1 tablespoon olive oil
½ pound ground beef
¼ pound Italian sausage
½ cup onion, chopped
2 cloves garlic, minced
1 - 28 ounce can crushed tomatoes
2 tablespoons Italian seasonings
1 teaspoon salt
1 teaspoon sugar

Hot cooked GF spaghetti noodles
Parmesan cheese

In a large sauce pan, brown the meats in the olive oil over medium-high heat. Add the onion and garlic and cook for several minutes longer until the onions are soft. Add the remaining ingredients, bring to a boil, and serve over hot cooked noodles. Pass the parmesan cheese at the table.

Total carbs 60g - not including noodles

❖ Spaghetti and Meatballs:

Increase the ground beet to **1 pound** and skip the sausage. In a medium bowl, add ½ **cup chopped onion, 1 teaspoon salt** and ½ **teaspoon pepper** to the beef and mix well. Form into 1 inch meatballs and fry in the oil over medium-high heat until cooked through and browned on all sides. Add the sauce ingredients, onion through sugar, to the pan and bring to a boil. Serve over noodles.

Super Easy Crock Pot Roast

2-3 pound roast
2 cups water

Cut the roast into 1 inch thick slices. Place the meat in the crock pot. Cover the meat with the water and cook on high for 4 hours or low for 6-8 hours.

Gravy:
3 tablespoons of flour
¼ cup water
1 teaspoon salt
½ teaspoon pepper

Remove the meat and pour the broth into a medium sauce pan. Place the pan over medium-high heat on the stove. In a small bowl, mix together the flour and water until smooth. When the broth is boiling, whisk the flour mixture slowly into the broth until it's the right consistency. Add the salt and pepper.

❖ Pot Roast

Two hours before the roast is done, add **4 peeled and cubed potatoes** and **2 cups carrots, chopped,** along with **2 cups boiling water**. Continue to cook for the remaining two hours. Make gravy with the liquid once cooking is done, if desired.

Total carbs Meat 0g
Gravy 18g

Swiss Steak

½ cup flour
1 teaspoon salt
1 pound thin sliced steak
2 tablespoons olive oil

1 tablespoon olive oil
½ cup onion, thinly sliced
2 cloves garlic, minced

1 - 16 ounce can crushed tomatoes
Mozzarella slices

Mix the flour and salt in a small bowl. On a cutting board, sprinkle a slice of steak on both sides with a little of the flour mixture. Using a meat tenderizing mallet, pound the flour into the steak on both sides until the meat is about ¼ inch thick. Place the beef slice on a plate and repeat with the remaining slices. Heat the olive oil in a large frying pan. Cook the beef, in several batches, if needed, over medium-high heat until done. Remove and keep warm.

Add the remaining 1 tablespoon olive oil, onions, and garlic to the pan. Sauté until tender. Add the crushed tomatoes and heat through. Return the beef to the pan, mix it into the tomato sauce and cook for several minutes until the beef is reheated. Top each piece of beef with a slice of mozzarella cheese. Cover and remove from heat. Allow to stand until the cheese is melted, then serve.

Total carbs 85g

Szechwan Stir-fry *

1 tablespoon oil
1 pound beef, thinly sliced

1 clove garlic, minced
2 carrots, thinly sliced
4 green onions, chopped
3 teaspoons grated gingerroot

4 tablespoons GF soy sauce
4 tablespoons white wine
1 tablespoon cornstarch
¼ cup water
1 tablespoon spicy Asian sauce
1 teaspoon sugar
¼ - ½ teaspoon cayenne pepper

Hot cooked rice

Place the oil in a large frying pan or wok. Brown the meat in batches in the oil. Add the veggies, garlic through ginger, to the last batch of meat. Cook until the veggies are crisp tender, stirring occasionally. While the meat is cooking, mix the remaining ingredients in a small bowl, soy sauce through cayenne pepper.

Add all the meat back into the pan once the last batch is done. Add the soy sauce mixture to the pan or wok. Cook until thickened. Serve with hot cooked rice.

Total carbs 30g - not including rice

 194

Tacos *

1 pound ground beef
½ cup onion, chopped
2 cloves garlic, crushed
½ cup salsa
2 tablespoons chili powder
2 teaspoons coriander
1½ teaspoons ground cumin
Tabasco sauce to taste

Toppings:
Salsa
2 large tomatoes, chopped
Lettuce, finely sliced
Shredded cheddar cheese
Taco shells

Brown the beef in a medium frying pan over medium-high heat. Add the onion and garlic and cook until tender. Add the salsa and seasonings. Heat through. Serve inside the taco shells with extra salsa, tomato, lettuce, and cheese.

Total carbs 20g - not including toppings or shells

Tex-Mex Chili*

½ pound ground beef
2 cloves garlic, minced
½ cup onion, chopped
½ cup red bell pepper, chopped
½ cup carrot, diced
1 - 8 ounce can tomato sauce
½ cup corn
1 cup salsa
1 - 15 ounce can black beans,
    drained and rinsed
1 tablespoon chili powder

1 teaspoon cumin
1 teaspoon salt
½ teaspoon cayenne pepper
½ teaspoon oregano

Hot cooked GF noodles

Toppings:
Shredded cheddar cheese
Sour cream

In a medium sauce pan, brown the ground beef, adding the garlic, onion, carrots, and peppers when it's almost done. Cook until the veggies are tender. Add the remaining ingredients, tomato sauce through oregano, and simmer for 15-30 minutes. Serve over noodles with a generous helping of shredded cheese on top and a dollop of sour cream.

Total carbs 120g - not including noodles

Volcano Meatballs *

(A hit with the kids)

¼ cup onion, chopped
1 clove garlic, minced
3 tablespoons ketchup
1 teaspoon prepared mustard
1 teaspoon salt
¼ teaspoon pepper
1 pound lean ground beef

12 –½ inch cheddar cheese squares
2 cups marinara sauce

Preheat the oven to 350° and grease a 9x9 pan. Mix the first 6 ingredients in a medium bowl, onion through pepper. Add the ground beef and mix well. Form 12 meatballs, placing a cheese square in the center of each one. Place the meatballs in the prepared pan and bake for 20-25 minutes. Serve with marinara sauce over the meatballs.

Total carbs 70g

Notes:

Notes:

Chicken Recipes

Any recipe with an * is one that can be made in about 30 minutes

Andy's Enchilada Hot Dish

3 tablespoons butter
½ cup onion, chopped
1 clove garlic, minced
3 tablespoons flour
1 cup milk
2 - 8 ounce cans tomato sauce
1 cup salsa
2 green chilies, chopped
1 teaspoon salt

¼ teaspoon pepper
¼ teaspoon cayenne pepper
2 cups cooked chicken, shredded

5 GF tortillas (see page 21)
2 cups grated cheddar cheese

Sour cream

Preheat the oven to 350° and grease a 2.5 quart casserole dish. In a medium sauce pan, brown the onions and garlic in the butter until tender. Stir in the flour until mixed well and then add the milk and tomato sauce. Continue cooking until thick, stirring frequently. Add all the remaining ingredients except the cheese and tortillas. Heat through.

In the prepared pan, layer one tortilla, ¾ cup sauce, and a sprinkling of cheese. Repeat five times. Spread any remaining cheese on top. Cover with foil and bake for 30 minutes. Serve with sour cream.

Total carbs 220g

Artichoke Chicken Bake *

1½ pounds chicken tenders
3 tablespoons butter

1 – 6 ounce jar marinated artichoke hearts,
drained
½ cup mushrooms, sliced
½ cup onion, thinly sliced
1 clove garlic, minced

⅓ cup flour
1 teaspoon Italian seasonings
1 teaspoon salt
½ teaspoon pepper
1½ cups chicken broth
½ cup white wine

Hot cooked GF noodles

Preheat the oven to 350°. Melt the butter in a large frying pan and brown the outside of the chicken tenders. Place them in a 9x13 baking pan. Add the artichokes, mushrooms, onions, and garlic to the pan and sauté in the butter for 2-3 minutes.

Add the flour, Italian seasonings, salt, and pepper to the pan. Mix well. Then add the chicken broth and wine. Cook, stirring well, until the sauce is thick and bubbly. Spoon the sauce over the chicken and bake for 15-20 minutes or until the chicken is done. Serve over hot cooked noodles.

Total carbs 52g - not including noodles

Blackberry Balsamic Chicken *

2 tablespoons olive oil
½ cup onion, thinly sliced

1½ pounds chicken tenders
1 teaspoon Italian seasonings
½ teaspoon salt

⅓ cup blackberry jam
3 tablespoons balsamic vinegar
½ teaspoon salt
½ teaspoon pepper

Heat the oil in a large frying pan over medium-high heat. Add the onions and sauté for 5 minutes.

Sprinkle the chicken with the Italian seasonings and salt. Add the chicken to the pan and cook until it's no longer pink in the middle. Add the jam, vinegar, salt, and pepper. Cook until the preserves have melted, coating the chicken with the sauce.

Total carbs 85g

Brown Rice Chicken Casserole

4 slices of bacon
1½ pounds chicken
½ cup onion, chopped
½ cup celery, chopped
½ cup mushrooms, chopped
2 tablespoons Worcestershire sauce
1 teaspoon salt
½ teaspoon pepper
½ teaspoon sage
1½ cups brown rice, uncooked
3½ cups hot chicken broth

1 cup grated cheddar cheese

Cook the bacon in a medium frying pan until done. Remove the bacon and sauté the veggies in the bacon drippings for a few minutes. Place the veggies, crumbled bacon, and all the remaining ingredients except the cheese into a crock pot. Cook on low for 3-4 hours or until the rice is done. Add cheese just before serving.

Total carbs 80g - including rice

Chicken Basil Stir Fry *

2 tablespoons oil
1 pound chicken tenders
1 teaspoon salt

1 cup chicken broth
1 teaspoon ground ginger
½ teaspoon cayenne pepper
1 tablespoon fish sauce *or* GF soy sauce
1 tablespoon flour

2 tablespoons fresh chives, chopped
2 cloves garlic, minced

2 cups lightly packed fresh basil leaves, coarsely chopped

Hot cooked rice

Place the oil in a large frying pan and add the chicken, sprinkling it with salt. Cook until the chicken is done. While it's cooking, mix the chicken broth, ginger, cayenne pepper, fish or soy sauce, and the flour in a small bowl. Remove the chicken from the heat and allow to cool just a little.

While it's cooling, add the chives and garlic to the pan and cook for 1 minute. Add the broth mixture and cook until thick and bubbly. Cut up the chicken into small slices. Add the chicken back to the pan along with the basil. Cook until just heated through, about one minute. Serve with rice.

Total carbs 12g - not including rice

Chicken with Caramelized Onions *

8 strips of bacon
1 cup onions, thinly sliced
8 large chicken tenders
¼ teaspoon garlic salt
¼ teaspoon lemon pepper
¼ cup brown sugar
¾ cup shredded cheddar cheese

In a large frying pan, cook the bacon. When it's done, set aside and keep warm. Pour out most of the bacon grease. Add the onions to the pan. Sauté for about 5 minutes. Sprinkle the chicken with garlic salt and lemon pepper and add to the onions in the pan.

Cook until the chicken is done and remove just the chicken. Keep warm on a serving platter. Add the brown sugar to the onions in the pan. Cook a few minutes longer until the brown sugar has dissolved. Place the chicken back in the pan. Place a strip of bacon on each chicken tender. Top evenly with onions and cheese. Allow the cheese to melt before serving.

Total carbs 70g

Chicken and Mushroom Fettuccine *

2 tablespoons olive oil
1 pound chicken tenders
1 teaspoon salt
½ teaspoon pepper

¼ cup butter
½ cup onion, chopped
¼ cup mushrooms, sliced
2 cloves garlic, minced
4 ounces cream cheese

2 tablespoons flour
1½ cups milk
2 tablespoons white wine
½ cup parmesan cheese
½ teaspoon salt
¼ teaspoon cayenne pepper
¼ teaspoon chili powder
¼ teaspoon nutmeg

12 ounces GF spinach spaghetti noodles

Cook the noodles according to the package directions.

Spread the olive oil in a large frying pan and sauté the chicken tenders until done, sprinkling them with salt and pepper. Remove them from the pan and allow to cool slightly. Add the butter, onion, mushrooms, and garlic to the pan and cook until tender. Stir in the cream cheese until melted. Then mix in the flour well and add the milk. Whisk until smooth.

Add the remaining sauce ingredients, wine through nutmeg, and bring to a boil, stirring often. Cut the chicken into chunks and add to the sauce. Pour the sauce over the spinach noodles and serve.

Total carbs 40g - not including noodles
About 8g carbs per ½ cup serving of sauce

Chicken with Creamy Mustard Sauce *

2 tablespoons olive oil
1 pound chicken tenders
1 teaspoon salt
½ teaspoon pepper

1 teaspoon flour
½ cup milk

¼ cup white wine

2 tablespoons prepared honey Dijon mustard
1 teaspoon tarragon

In a large frying pan, sauté the chicken in the olive oil, sprinkling with salt and pepper. When cooked through, remove the chicken from the pan and keep warm on a serving plate. In a small bowl, mix the flour and milk until dissolved. Set aside.

Add the wine to the pan and cook over high heat until half of it has evaporated. Add the milk mixture, mustard, and tarragon to the pan and cook until thickened. Pour any juice from the chicken into the pan and mix. Then pour the mustard sauce over the chicken and serve.

Total carbs 10g

Chicken Pizza

1 batch of pizza dough (see pages 26-27)

Vinegar Sauce:
2 tablespoons balsamic vinegar
1½ tablespoons prepared mustard
2 teaspoons garlic, minced

Cheese Mixture:
¾ cup mozzarella cheese
¼ cup feta cheese
¼ cup parmesan cheese

Other Toppings:
1 cup fresh tomatoes, chopped
½ cup mushrooms
¼ cup onions
1½ cups cooked, shredded chicken

Preheat the oven to 350° and grease a medium pizza pan. Make the crust according to the directions, or use a store-bought crust. Mix the vinegar sauce ingredients in a small bowl, the cheese mixture ingredients in a medium bowl and cut up whatever other toppings you would like to add. (Cook some chicken in olive oil with a sprinkle of salt and pepper if you don't already have shredded chicken).

Spread the shredded chicken and other toppings evenly over the crust. Then sprinkle with the cheese mixture. Drizzle the vinegar sauce evenly over the pizza and bake for about 15 minutes.

Total carbs depends on the crust used
About 10g for toppings

Chicken in a Pot

1 -3 pound whole chicken (a small one)
1 teaspoon salt
¼ teaspoon thyme
¼ teaspoon tarragon
¼ teaspoon celery salt
¼ teaspoon pepper

Preheat the oven to 400°. Line a 2.5 quart lidded casserole dish with foil. Combine the spices and sprinkle them over the chicken. Place the chicken in the pot and cover tightly. Bake for 1½ hours or until done.

For gravy:

If there are juices in the bottom of the pan after cooking, pour them into a small sauce pan, add **1 cup of water** and bring to a boil. Mix **1 tablespoon flour** with **3 tablespoons water**. Thicken the broth with the flour mixture by whisking it into the boiling broth until desired consistency. Add **salt** and **pepper** to taste.

Total carbs 0g

Chicken Tikka

Marinade:
1 inch piece of fresh garlic, grated
3 cloves garlic, minced
1 tablespoon lemon juice
½ cup plain yogurt
1 tablespoon oil
½ teaspoon chili powder
½ teaspoon salt

1½ pounds chicken tenders

Onions:
2 tablespoons oil
1 tablespoon lemon juice
½ teaspoon cumin
¼ teaspoon turmeric
½ teaspoon salt
2 onions, slivered

3 limes, quartered

In a large bowl, mix the marinade ingredients. Add the chicken and refrigerate at least 1 hour. Meanwhile, mix the oil, lemon juice, cumin, turmeric, and salt in a large bowl and add the onions.

Cover a cookie sheet with foil and spread the onions on the sheet. Broil for about 10 minutes until cooked through and slightly browned, stirring once.

Remove the chicken from the marinade and sauté in a large frying pan until golden brown. Serve the chicken topped with onions and a squeeze of fresh lime juice.

Total carbs 15g

Chicken with Wine Sauce

1 teaspoon Italian seasoning
1 teaspoon salt
½ teaspoon pepper
1 tablespoon olive oil
1½ pounds boneless, skinless chicken
½ cup white wine
½ cup chicken broth
½ cup mushrooms
¾ cup carrots, shredded

3 tablespoons flour
3 tablespoons water

3 tablespoons sour cream

Sprinkle the chicken with the Italian seasonings, salt, and pepper. Spread the oil in a large skillet and sauté the chicken until it's almost done. Add the wine, chicken broth, and veggies. Cover and simmer for about 10 minutes. Meanwhile, mix the flour and water together. When the veggies are tender, stir in the flour mixture and cook until the liquid thickens. Remove from heat, stir in the sour cream.

Total carbs 20g

Chimichangas *

1½ pounds chicken
1 cup chicken broth
2 cloves garlic, minced
2 tablespoons chili powder
1 tablespoon oregano
1 tablespoon vinegar
1 teaspoon salt
1 teaspoon cumin
¼ teaspoon cayenne pepper

Toppings:
GF flour tortillas (see page 21)
Salsa
Sour cream
Cheese
Lettuce

In a medium sauce pan, boil the chicken in the broth until it's cooked through. Remove from heat and shred the chicken, saving the broth in a small bowl. While the chicken is cooking, combine the remaining ingredients, garlic through cayenne, in a small bowl. Add them to the now empty sauce pan along with the shredded chicken. Mix well and cook over medium-high heat until the chicken is heated through. Add enough reserved broth to moisten the chicken. Serve on tortillas with salsa, sour cream, cheese or whatever other fillings you want.

Total carbs for the chicken 0g
About 24g carbs per tortilla plus carbs for toppings

Coconut Chicken *

1 cup frozen orange juice concentrate
1 egg, beaten

1 cup GF bread crumbs
¾ cup grated coconut
½ teaspoon salt
1 teaspoon curry powder

1½ pounds chicken tenders

¼ cup butter, melted

Preheat the oven to 350° and grease a 9x9 baking pan. In a small bowl, mix the orange juice concentrate and the egg. In another small bowl, mix the bread crumbs, coconut, curry powder and salt. Dip the chicken pieces in the orange mixture and then coat with the bread crumbs.

Arranged the chicken pieces in the pan and drizzle the melted butter over the top. Bake for 25-30 minutes or until the chicken is done.

Total carbs 100g

Cornflake Chicken *

1½ pounds boneless, skinless chicken breasts or tenders
½ cup mayonnaise, divided
1 cup crushed GF cornflakes, divided
1 teaspoon Italian seasoning, divided
1 teaspoon salt, divided
½ teaspoon pepper

Preheat the oven to 350°. Spread half of the mayonnaise in the bottom of a 9x13 cake pan. Sprinkle half the cornflakes, half the Italian seasonings, and half the salt over the mayonnaise.

Place the chicken pieces in the pan and spread the remaining half of the mayonnaise on the chicken. Then sprinkle with the remaining cornflakes, Italian seasonings, salt and the pepper. Bake for 25-30 minutes or until the chicken is done.

Total carbs 35g

Cranberry Chicken *

1 tablespoon olive oil
1 pound chicken tenders
1 teaspoon salt
½ teaspoon pepper
1 cup chicken broth
½ cup white wine
½ cup orange juice

3 tablespoons brown sugar
2 teaspoons prepared mustard
1 cup cranberries

1 tablespoon flour
3 tablespoons cold water

Spread the olive oil in a large frying pan. Sprinkle the chicken with salt and pepper, and sauté it until done. Remove the chicken from the pan and keep warm on a serving platter. Add the broth, wine, orange juice, brown sugar, mustard, and cranberries and bring to a boil.

Cook for a few minutes until the cranberries are soft. In a small bowl, mix the flour and water until dissolved. Stir in the flour mixture and cook until the sauce thickens. Pour the sauce over the chicken and serve.

Total carbs 12g

Creamy Thai Baked Chicken

Marinade:
1½ pounds chicken tenders
1 teaspoon Dijon mustard
1 jalapeño pepper, diced
3 tablespoons sherry

2 tablespoons butter

1 cup red bell pepper, coarsely chopped
1 cup zucchini, sliced

Sauce:
⅓ cup white wine
1 - 14 ounce can coconut milk
1 jalapeño pepper, diced
1 teaspoon salt
½ teaspoon pepper

Hot cooked rice

Mix all the marinade ingredients and refrigerate for several hours. Preheat the oven to 400°. Remove the chicken from the marinade and sauté it in a medium skillet in the butter until cooked through. Grease a 2.5 quart casserole dish. Place the chicken in the dish and top with the peppers and zucchinis.

In a small bowl, mix the sauce ingredients and pour into the skillet used for the chicken. Cook until warm, scraping up the browned bits. Pour the sauce over the chicken and bake for 20-25 minutes. Serve over hot cooked rice.

Total carbs 30g - not including rice

Crock Pot Orange Chicken

8 boneless skinless chicken thighs
2 tablespoons flour

½ cup orange marmalade
⅓ cup barbecue sauce
2 tablespoons GF soy sauce
¼ cup chicken broth
1 teaspoon ground ginger

Grease the crock pot. Add the chicken and sprinkle the flour over it, stirring to coat. In a small bowl, combine the marmalade, barbecue sauce, soy sauce, broth, and ginger. Pour this mixture over the chicken and cook on high for 2 hours, or on low for 3-4 hours.

Total carbs 160g

Curried Apricot Chicken

¼ cup flour
2 teaspoons curry powder
2 teaspoons salt
1½ pounds chicken tenders
2 tablespoons olive oil

2 tablespoons brown sugar
1 teaspoon GF chicken bouillon

½ cup onion, chopped
1 – 16 ounce can apricot halves, divided
2 tablespoons lemon juice
1 tablespoon GF soy sauce

1 tablespoon cornstarch
3 tablespoons water

Preheat the oven to 350° and grease a 9x13 pan. In a medium bowl, mix the flour, curry powder, and salt. Coat the chicken with the flour mixture. Heat the oil in a large frying pan and brown the chicken on both sides. Drain the apricots, reserving the liquid. Stir together the brown sugar, bouillon, onion, juice from the apricots, lemon juice, and soy sauce.

Place the chicken in the prepared pan. Add the liquid mixture to the frying pan and heat through, scraping the pan to incorporate drippings. Once this is boiling, pour it over the chicken and bake for 20-25 minutes, or until the chicken is done.

Remove the chicken from the pan, place on a serving platter and keep warm. Add the pan juices back into the frying pan. Mix the cornstarch and water and slowly whisk them into the pan juices once they are boiling. Add just enough to make a thick sauce. Add the apricots halves to the frying pan and heat through. Pour over the chicken and serve.

Total carbs 200g

Curried BBQ Chicken

¼ cup oil
Zest of 1 lime
Juice of 1 lime
1 tablespoon grated onion
1 clove garlic, minced
1 teaspoon curry powder
½ teaspoon salt
½ teaspoon cumin
½ teaspoon coriander
¼ teaspoon cinnamon
¼ teaspoon pepper
1½ pounds chicken tenders

1 lime, sliced
Parsley

In a large bowl, combine the oil through pepper. Then add the chicken tenders. Marinate for 4-6 hours. Barbeque the chicken until done, basting with the marinade at the end. Garnish with lime slices and parsley, if desired.

Total carbs 0g

Enchilada Chicken Pizza

1 recipe of pizza crust (see pages 26-27)

⅔ cup onion, chopped
1 tablespoon oil
2 cups cooked, shredded chicken
2 green chilies, chopped
2 tablespoons taco seasoning
½ teaspoon garlic powder

¾ cup enchilada sauce
2 cups shredded mozzarella cheese or Mexican cheese blend

Preheat the oven to 350° and grease a medium pizza pan. Prepare the crust according to the recipe. Sauté the onions in the oil in a medium sauce pan until tender. Add the chicken, chilies, taco seasoning, and garlic powder. Spread the enchilada sauce over the crust. Top with half the cheese and the chicken mixture, followed by the other half of the cheese. Bake for 15-20 minutes or until the cheese is melted.

Total carbs depends on the crust used
About 10g for toppings

Fiesta Chicken Burritos

1 tablespoon oil
1 medium onion, sliced
1 red bell pepper, chopped
1½ cups cooked, shredded chicken
1 - 15 ounce can whole corn, drained
1 - 15 ounce can black beans, drained & rinsed
1 - 10 ounce can diced tomatoes, undrained
2 jalapeño peppers, seeded and chopped
3 tablespoons cumin
1 teaspoon salt

1 teaspoon paprika
½ teaspoon pepper
½ teaspoon garlic powder
¼ teaspoon cayenne pepper
¼ teaspoon crushed red pepper flakes

4 ounces cream cheese

3 cup shredded cheddar cheese, divided
6 GF tortillas (see page 21)
Sour cream

Preheat the oven to 350°. Grease a 9x13 pan. Sauté the onions and bell pepper in the oil in a large frying pan until tender. Add the remaining burrito ingredients, chicken through pepper flakes.

Add the cream cheese and mix well. Place ¾ cup of the chicken mixture into each tortilla with ¼ cup cheese. Roll the tortilla and place it in the prepared pan. Top with cheese and foil, and bake for 20-30 minutes. Serve with sour cream.

Total carbs 310g
About 50g carbs per tortilla

Fiery Chicken Stir Fry *

1½ pounds chicken
½ cup flour
¼ - ½ cup oil

Sauce:
1 teaspoon garlic
¼ cup green onions
2 teaspoons chicken bouillon
3 tablespoons sugar

3 tablespoons vinegar
¾ teaspoon cayenne pepper
1 teaspoon red curry paste
2 tablespoons sesame seeds
¼ cup GF soy sauce
2 tablespoons flour

Hot cooked rice

Cut the chicken into 1 inch pieces and coat in the flour. Add 3-4 tablespoons of oil to a hot wok or heavy frying pan. Fry the coated chicken in batches until golden brown and cooked through. Add more oil if needed. As you remove each batch, keep the chicken warm. Mix the sauce ingredients in a small bowl while the chicken is cooking.

Once all the chicken is done, add the sauce to the now empty pan and cook until thick and bubbly. Return the chicken to the pan. Cook a few minutes longer until the chicken is heated through. Serve with rice.

Total carbs 115g - not including rice
About 7g carbs per piece of chicken

Glazed Ginger Chicken *

1 tablespoon olive oil
1 pound chicken tenders
1 teaspoon salt
½ teaspoon pepper

1 tablespoon cornstarch
½ cup chicken broth

¼ cup brown sugar
2 tablespoons honey Dijon mustard
2 tablespoons honey
1 teaspoon ground ginger

Sprinkle the chicken with salt and pepper. In a large frying pan, sauté the chicken in the olive oil until done. Mix the cornstarch into the chicken broth and add it to the pan along with the remaining ingredients. Heat through and serve.

Total carbs 95g
About 20g carbs per tender

Indian Chicken Patties *

(Mediterranean Cucumber salad goes well with this dish, see page 331)

Patties:
1½ pounds ground chicken
3 green onions, finely chopped
2 tablespoons lemon juice
1 tablespoon paprika
2 teaspoons cumin
1 teaspoon ground ginger
½ teaspoon ground cardamom
½ teaspoon salt
¼ teaspoon cayenne pepper
¼ teaspoon black pepper

2 tablespoons oil

Yogurt Sauce:
½ cup plain yogurt
½ teaspoon cumin
1 teaspoon salt
½ teaspoon pepper

In a large bowl, combine all the patty ingredients and mix well. Form patties out of the chicken. Add the oil to a large skillet. Fry the patties over medium-high heat until cooked through, flipping once. While the patties are cooking, mix the yogurt sauce ingredients in a small bowl. Serve with the yogurt sauce.

Total carbs 0g
About 1g carbs per tablespoon of sauce

Kaia's Spiced Chicken *

⅓ cup flour
1 tablespoon cilantro
¼ teaspoon cayenne pepper
¼ teaspoon crushed red pepper flakes
¼ teaspoon onion powder
¼ teaspoon garlic salt
1 teaspoon salt ½ teaspoon pepper

2 tablespoons olive oil
2 tablespoons lemon juice

Cilantro
Crushed red pepper flakes

1 ½ pounds chicken tenders

In a medium bowl, mix the flour through pepper. Dredge the chicken in the flour mixture and sauté in the olive oil in a large frying pan until done, adding the lemon juice while it's cooking. Cook until the lemon juice has evaporated. Garnish with cilantro and red pepper flakes if desired.

Total carbs 30 g

Lemon Basil Chicken *

Marinade:
½ cup fresh basil, chopped
¼ cup fresh chives, chopped
3 tablespoons lemon juice
½ teaspoon lemon pepper
¼ teaspoon pepper
1 pound chicken tenders

Basil topping:
¼ cup fresh basil, finely chopped
2 tablespoons mayonnaise
1 tablespoon lemon juice
1 teaspoon Dijon mustard
1 clove garlic, minced
½ teaspoon olive oil

2 tablespoons olive oil

In a shallow bowl, combine the marinade ingredients and add the chicken. Allow to sit for at least 15 minutes. While the chicken is marinating, mix together all the ingredients for the basil topping in a small bowl. Set aside. Heat the remaining 2 tablespoons olive oil in a large frying pan. Discard the marinade and add the chicken to the pan. Cook until no longer pink in the middle. Serve the chicken with a dollop of basil topping on each piece.

Total carbs 10g

Lemon Roasted Chicken

6-8 carrots, peeled and cut into thirds
3 stalks celery, cut into thirds
1 onion, cut in wedges
1 whole chicken, rinsed and patted dry
1½ tablespoons salt
2 teaspoons pepper

4 garlic cloves, minced
1 teaspoon thyme
1 teaspoon rosemary
¼ cup butter, softened

1 lemon, halved
2 bay leaves

½ cup chicken broth
1 tablespoon flour
½ cup white wine

Preheat the oven to 450°. Line a 9x13 pan with foil. Grease the foil. Spread the carrots, celery, and onions in the pan. Season the chicken both inside and out with the salt and pepper. In a small bowl, combine the garlic, herbs, and butter. Rub the chicken both inside and out with the butter mixture and place on top of the veggies in the roasting pan. Squeeze the lemon halves over the chicken and place the rinds inside the chicken, along with the bay leaves.

Place the pan in the oven and cook for 1¼ -1½ hours or until meat thermometer reads 180° in the thigh. Transfer the chicken to a serving platter and the veggies to a bowl.

For the gravy, pour the drippings from the pan and from inside the chicken into a medium sauce pan, scraping up the bits from the bottom of the roasting pan. Whisk the chicken broth with the flour and wine. Slowly add it to the boiling drippings until desired thickness.

Total carbs 0g for chicken
About 5g carbs per ½ cup serving of veggies

Maple Glazed Chicken

2 pounds bone-in chicken pieces
2 teaspoons salt - divided
½ teaspoon pepper - divided
2 teaspoons fresh thyme, chopped
⅓ cup maple syrup
1 tablespoon oil
2 tablespoons balsamic vinegar
¼ teaspoon cayenne pepper

Preheat the oven to 400°. Line a 9x13 pan with foil. Grease the foil. Rub the chicken pieces with half the salt, half the pepper, and the thyme. Arrange them in the pan. In a small bowl, mix together the remaining salt and pepper along with the maple syrup, oil, vinegar, and cayenne pepper. Pour this over the chicken and bake for 45-50 minutes, basting occasionally with the pan juices. Remove the chicken to a serving platter and pour some of the pan juices over the chicken before serving.

Total carbs 40g

Mexican Chicken Skillet *

1 teaspoon garlic salt
½ teaspoon pepper
1 pound chicken tenders
1 tablespoon oil
1½ cups salsa
1 - 15 ounce can black beans, drained and rinsed
1½ cup shredded cheddar cheese

Sprinkle the chicken with garlic salt and pepper. In a large frying pan, sauté the chicken in the oil until cooked through. Add the salsa and beans. Simmer for 5 minutes until heated through. Top with cheese and serve.

Total carbs 100g

Mexican Rice Bowls

Marinade:
2 chipotle chilies in adobo sauce
1 teaspoon black pepper
2 teaspoons cumin
2 teaspoons oregano
4 garlic cloves
½ onion, quartered
¼ cup oil

2 pounds chicken tenders

Toppings:
Shredded cheddar cheese
Sour cream
Salsa
Shredded lettuce

Place all the marinade ingredients in a blender and puree until smooth. Coat the chicken with the marinade and refrigerate at least one hour or overnight.

Barbeque the chicken until done and cut into strips.

Serve in a bowl with: Rice Bowl Guacamole, Rice Bowl Lime Rice, Rice Bowl Black Beans, cheese, sour cream, salsa, and lettuce. (See pages 336-337)

Total carbs 0g - not including sides and toppings

Molasses Baked Chicken *

¼ cup chives or green onions, chopped
¼ cup GF soy sauce
¼ cup red wine
3 tablespoons molasses
1 tablespoon oil
½ teaspoon ground cumin
¼ teaspoon cayenne pepper
1½ pounds chicken tenders

Preheat the oven to 350° and grease a 9x13 pan. Mix all ingredients except the chicken in a small bowl. Arrange the chicken in the pan. Pour the sauce over the top and bake for 25-30 minutes, or until the chicken is cooked through.

Total carbs 45g

Mozzarella Stuffed Chicken Rolls

8 boneless, skinless chicken breasts,
3 cups shredded mozzarella cheese- divided

1 cup GF bread crumbs
2 teaspoons Italian seasonings
3 tablespoons parmesan cheese
½ teaspoon garlic powder
½ teaspoon salt

½ teaspoon cumin
½ teaspoon pepper
½ cup butter, melted

1 tablespoon butter
1 tablespoon flour
1 cup milk

Preheat the oven to 400° and grease a 9x13 pan. Pound each chicken breast to about ½ inch thick. Place 3 tablespoons of mozzarella cheese on each flattened chicken breast and roll it up. Secure each roll with a toothpick. Mix the bread crumbs with the Italian seasonings, parmesan cheese, garlic powder, salt, cumin, and pepper. In a small bowl, melt the ½ cup of butter.

Dip the chicken rolls in the melted butter and then in the bread crumb mixture. Place the rolls in the pan, but don't crowd them. Drizzle any remaining melted butter used for dipping over the chicken. Bake for 30-35 minutes.

While it's baking, melt the 1 tablespoon of butter in a small sauce pan. When it's melted, add the flour and mix well. Whisk in the milk until smooth and cook until it's thick and bubbly. Add any remaining mozzarella cheese. Serve the chicken with the cheese sauce drizzled over the top.

Total carbs 75g

Opa's Fried Chicken

¼ cup oil

1 cup flour
¼ cup cornflakes, crushed (optional)
2 teaspoons paprika
2 teaspoons salt
¼ teaspoon pepper

1 cut up fryer chicken or 3-4 pounds of bone in chicken pieces

½ cup milk
Additional flour
½ cup water
1 teaspoon salt ½ teaspoon pepper

Heat the oil in a large frying pan. Combine the flour through the pepper in a shallow bowl and coat the chicken pieces. Add them to the pan and cook over medium-high heat for about 6-8 minutes. Turn the pieces over, cover, and cook for 40 minutes over low heat. Flip the pieces again and cook uncovered for another 10 minutes.

Add more flour to the remaining coating mixture until there is about 3 tablespoons all together. Add the milk and whisk until smooth. When the chicken is done, remove it to a serving platter and keep warm.

For the gravy:
Increase the heat to medium-high and add the water to the pan drippings, scraping to loosen all the browned bits. When it comes to a boil, add the milk mixture a little at a time, and whisk until it thickens. Add additional **1 teaspoon salt** and ½ **teaspoon pepper**. Serve with mashed potatoes.

15-20g carbs per piece

Opa's Fried Chicken Nuggets

1 cup flour
¼ cup cornflakes, crushed (optional)
2 teaspoons paprika
2 teaspoons salt
¼ teaspoon pepper

2 pounds boneless chicken
3 tablespoons oil

In a medium, shallow bowl mix the flour through pepper. Cut the chicken into 1 inch pieces and coat in the flour mixture. In a large frying pan, heat the oil. Add the chicken pieces and cook, stirring occasionally until browned on all sided and cooked through.

To make nuggets along with the Opa's Fried Chicken recipe, cut up **1 pound of boneless chicken**. Coat the pieces in the flour mix and add to the pan during the last 10 minutes of cooking, flipping once.

5g carbs per chicken nugget

Orange-Glazed Chicken Tenders *

1 tablespoon olive oil
1½ pounds chicken tenders
1 teaspoon salt
½ teaspoon pepper

2 tablespoons flour
1 teaspoon prepared mustard
¾ cup orange juice
¼ cup orange marmalade
2 tablespoons GF soy sauce

Sprinkle the tenders with salt and pepper. In a large frying pan, sauté them in the olive oil until done. Meanwhile, mix the remaining ingredients in a small bowl. When the tenders are done, add the sauce and cook until thickened.

For Fun: Try using apricot or peach preserves instead of the orange marmalade.

Total carbs 80g

Overnight Spiced Chicken

½ cup orange juice
2 tablespoons olive oil
2 tablespoons GF soy sauce
1 tablespoon honey
2 teaspoons garlic powder
2 teaspoons onion powder
1 teaspoon salt

1 teaspoon sage
1 teaspoon thyme
1 teaspoon allspice
½ teaspoon cinnamon
½ teaspoon black pepper
¼ teaspoon cayenne pepper
1½ pounds chicken tenders

In a shallow bowl with a lid, combine all the ingredients except the chicken and mix well. Add the chicken, coat it in the marinade, and refrigerate overnight. Grill or broil the chicken until no longer pink, about 10 minutes.

Total carbs 15g

Peanutty Indonesian Chicken Skewers *

Marinade:
2 cloves garlic, minced
1 tablespoon brown sugar
3 tablespoons GF soy sauce
Zest of 1 lime
Juice of half a lime
½ teaspoon ground ginger
¼ teaspoon cayenne pepper
1 pound boneless chicken breast, cut into thin slices, lengthwise

1 tablespoon sesame seeds

Peanut sauce:
3 tablespoons creamy peanut butter
1 tablespoon brown sugar
1½ tablespoons GF soy sauce
Juice of half a lime
½ teaspoon cayenne pepper
1 clove garlic, minced

In a shallow bowl, mix together the marinade ingredients and add the chicken to it. Allow it to sit for at least 20 minutes. Meanwhile, mix together the peanut sauce ingredients in a small bowl and set aside. Thread the chicken onto skewers. Sprinkle them with sesame seeds. Barbecue them until done or broil 4-5 minutes on each side. Serve with the peanut sauce for dipping.

Total carbs 47g - including sauce

Quick Italian Chicken *

1 pound chicken tenders
¼ cup Italian salad dressing
1¼ cups chicken broth
1 cup instant brown rice
¼ cup sliced almonds

Place chicken in a large frying pan and pour the Italian dressing over it. Cook over medium-high heat until the chicken is cooked through, turning at least once.

Remove the chicken and keep warm. Add the chicken broth to the pan and bring it to a boil. Add the rice and almonds. Simmer on low heat for 5-7 minutes. Serve the chicken over the rice.

Total carbs 70g - including rice

Ranch Chicken Skewers *

¼ cup olive oil
½ cup ranch dressing
3 tablespoons soy sauce
2 teaspoons lemon juice
1 tablespoon Italian seasonings
2 teaspoons salt
½ teaspoon pepper
1½ pounds chicken tenders, cut into 1 inch cubes

Mix all the ingredients in a medium bowl, stirring well to coat the chicken. Allow to marinate for 15 minutes or more. Place the chicken on skewers and broil or barbeque flipping once for about 8-10 minutes or until the chicken is done and slightly browned.

Total carbs 20g

Red Chicken *

1½ pounds chicken tenders

1 tablespoon flour
½ cup chicken broth
¼ cup brown sugar
¼ cup ketchup
3 tablespoons lemon juice
2 tablespoons soy sauce

½ cup onion, chopped
1 teaspoon prepared mustard
1 teaspoon paprika
1 teaspoon chili powder
½ teaspoon salt
¼ teaspoon pepper

Preheat the oven to 350°. Arrange the chicken pieces in a 9x13 baking pan. In a small sauce pan, whisk together the flour, broth, brown sugar, ketchup, lemon juice, and soy sauce. Bring to a boil and cook until thickened. Add the next 6 ingredients, onion through pepper, and pour over the chicken. Bake for 25-30 minutes.

Total carbs 90g
About 11g carbs per piece

Saucy Pesto Chicken *

1 tablespoon olive oil
1 pound chicken tenders
1 teaspoon salt
½ teaspoon pepper
1 - 8 ounce can tomato sauce
5 ounces basil pesto
⅓ cup parmesan cheese

Sprinkle the chicken with salt and pepper. In a large frying pan, cook the chicken in the olive oil until done. Add the pesto and tomato sauce, mixing well. Cook until heated through. Place the chicken and sauce in a serving dish and sprinkle with the parmesan cheese.

Total carbs 30g

Simple Parmesan Chicken

1 jar prepared spaghetti sauce
1 teaspoon Italian seasonings
¼ cup parmesan cheese
1½ pounds chicken tenders
2 cups mozzarella cheese

¼ cup parmesan cheese

Hot cooked noodles

Preheat the oven to 350°. Grease a 9x13 pan. Mix the parmesan cheese and the Italian spices into the spaghetti sauce and pour into the pan. Add the chicken and turn to coat. Bake uncovered for 35-40 minutes.

Remove from oven and top with remaining ¼ cup of parmesan cheese and the mozzarella cheese. Bake for another 5 minutes or until the cheese is melted. Serve with noodles.

Total carbs 120g
About 12g carbs per tender

Sweet and Spicy Mexican Chicken *

1 package taco seasoning
1½ pounds chicken tenders, cut into chunks
1 tablespoon oil
1 cup salsa
½ cup canned peaches, mashed

Hot cooked rice

Place the chicken pieces in a large bowl. Add the taco seasoning and mix to coat. Heat the oil in a large frying pan and add the chicken. Cook until the chicken is done. Add the salsa and the peaches, and cook until heated through. Serve over hot cooked rice.

Total carbs 42g - not including rice

Take-Out Lemon Chicken

2-4 tablespoons oil
1½ pounds chicken tenders
⅓ cup flour
½ teaspoon salt

3 tablespoons butter
¼ cup flour
1 cup lemon juice

1 cup chicken broth
⅓ cup sugar
1 teaspoon GF soy sauce

¼ cup fresh chives, chopped
One lemon cut into ½ inch chunks

Hot cooked rice

Heat 2 tablespoons of oil over medium-high heat in a wok or large frying pan. Cut the chicken into 1 inch pieces. Coat the chicken in the flour and sprinkle with salt. Cook in the hot oil in batches until it's done. Add more oil, if needed. Remove from the pan and keep warm.

Once all the chicken is done, add the butter to the pan. Once it's melted, add the ¼ cup flour and mix well. Then add the lemon juice, broth, sugar, and soy sauce and whisk until smooth. When it's thick and bubbly, stir in the chives, lemon pieces, and chicken. Serve over hot cooked rice.

Total carbs 150g - not including rice

Thai Chicken with Peanut Sauce *

1½ pounds chicken tenders
1 tablespoon oil
2 cloves garlic
1 teaspoon gingerroot, grated
1 cup onion, thinly sliced

2 cups chicken broth
2 tablespoons white wine
1½ tablespoons flour
1 tablespoon GF soy sauce
¼ teaspoon cayenne pepper
½ cup peanut butter

Hot cooked GF spaghetti/ linguini noodles

In a large frying pan, sauté the chicken tenders in the oil, adding the garlic, ginger and onion when the chicken is almost done. Cook until the veggies are tender and the chicken cooked through. Remove only the chicken, allow to cool slightly.

In a medium bowl, mix the broth through the peanut butter. Add to the onion mixture in the pan and cook until thick and bubbly. Cut the chicken pieces into slices and return to the sauce in the pan. Serve over cooked noodles.

Total carbs 16g- not including noodles

Thai Leek Stir Fry

1 pound of chicken, thinly sliced
3 tablespoons coconut oil - divided

2 leeks, chopped and cleaned
1 red bell pepper, chopped
½ cup mushrooms, chopped

2 inches of fresh ginger, grated
3 cloves garlic, minced
¼ cup lime juice
½ cup GF soy sauce
2 tablespoons honey
1 tablespoon Asian hot sauce
¼ cup fresh basil
¼ cup fresh cilantro

12 ounces GF spaghetti noodles, cooked

In a large frying pan, heat 2 tablespoons of the oil until very hot. Cook the chicken until slightly browned. Remove from pan and add the remaining tablespoon of oil. Add the leeks, bell pepper, and mushrooms and cook for several minutes until the leek are somewhat wilted.

Add the ginger, garlic, and lime juice. Return the chicken to pan. Cook for several more minutes. Add the remaining ingredients, soy sauce through cilantro, and cook a few minutes longer. Serve over noodles.

Total carbs 50g - not including noodles

Tip: *To clean leeks, cut in half lengthwise before chopping. Once chopped, place in a colander and rinse well to remove the sand.*

Tom Ka Chicken *

1 tablespoon oil
1½ pounds chicken, thinly sliced

½ cup onion, finely chopped
1 small zucchini, chopped
2 cloves garlic, minced
1½ teaspoons ground ginger

1 teaspoon green curry paste (or to taste)
1 – 14 ounce can coconut milk
¼ cup fresh basil
1 tablespoon brown sugar
1 teaspoon fish sauce

1 cup chicken broth
2 tablespoons flour

Hot cooked jasmine rice

In a large frying pan, cook the chicken in the oil over medium-high heat. When almost done, add the onion, zucchini, garlic, and ginger and sauté until soft. Add the remaining ingredients, mixing the flour in with the chicken broth before adding. Cook until it's thick and bubbly. Serve over rice.

Total carbs 49g - not including rice
About 6g carbs per ½ cup serving

Zesty Grilled Chicken

2 teaspoons lime juice
¼ cup oil
2 tablespoons red wine vinegar
1 tablespoon Worcestershire sauce
1 teaspoon salt
1 teaspoon sugar
1 teaspoon garlic salt
1 teaspoon onion powder
1 teaspoon paprika
1 teaspoon pepper
½ teaspoon crushed red pepper flakes
1½ pounds chicken tenders.

Mix all ingredients in a bowl and marinate for at least 2 hours. Grill chicken until done.

Total carbs 0g

Zucchini Boats *

5 medium zucchinis
1½ pounds ground chicken
1 tablespoon oil
½ cup onion, chopped
1 clove garlic, minced
1 cup Barbeque sauce
¼ teaspoon pepper
1 cup grated cheddar cheese, divided

Cut the zucchini in half lengthwise and scoop the seeds out. Place the zucchini in a microwave safe dish. Microwave on high for 3 minutes or until crisp tender. In a medium skillet, cook the chicken in the oil until done. Add the onion and garlic and cooking until tender.

Stir in the Barbeque sauce and half the cheese. Spoon about ¼ cup of the meat mixture into each zucchini shell. Microwave on high for 6 minutes. Sprinkle the rest of the cheese over the top and microwave for 2-3 minutes longer.

Total carbs 80g
About 10g carbs per boat

Notes:

Notes:

Pork and Sausage Recipes

Any recipe with an * is one that can be made in about 30 minutes

Apricot Pork Chops *

(This works with chicken as well)

1 tablespoon coconut oil
6 boneless pork chops
1 teaspoon salt
½ teaspoon pepper
3 slices of GF bread, crumbled
2 tablespoons apricot jam
2 tablespoons chives

Preheat the oven to 400° and grease a 9x13 inch pan. Place the bread crumbs in a small bowl and drizzle with the oil. Place the pork chops in the pan. Season with salt and pepper, and spread 1 teaspoon of jam on each one. Then sprinkle the bread crumbs and chives evenly over the top. Bake for 20-25 minutes or until the pork is cooked through and the bread is browned.

Total carbs 155g

BBQ Pork Sandwiches

(Easy, but not quick)

2 cups beef or chicken broth
2 pound pork roast, cut into thick slices
12 ounces barbeque sauce

Hamburger buns (see Basic White Bread variations, see page 15)

Place the broth and pork in a crock pot and cook on high for about 4 hours. Remove the pork and shred it using two forks. Pour the Barbeque sauce over it and place it in a shallow baking dish. Broil for about 5 minutes or until some of the top pieces begin to burn. Serve on buns or over hot cooked noodles.

Total carbs 170g - not including the buns

Crustless Spinach Quiche

6 eggs, beaten
1 teaspoon salt
½ teaspoon pepper
¼ teaspoon cayenne pepper
1 cup milk
½ pound sausage or ham, chopped
½ medium onion, chopped

2 cups frozen spinach,
    thawed and squeezed dry
½ cup of mushrooms, chopped
1 cup cheddar cheese
¾ cup cottage cheese
½ cup shredded Swiss cheese

Preheat the oven to 400° and grease a 2.5 quart casserole dish. In a large bowl, beat the eggs, then mix in the remaining ingredients. Pour the egg mixture into the prepared pan. Bake for 40-45 minutes.

Total carbs 60g

Ham Alfredo *

1 tablespoon olive oil
1½ cups ham, cubed
½ cup onion, chopped
2 cloves garlic, minced

1½ cups milk
2 ounces cream cheese
1 teaspoon salt
½ teaspoon pepper
1 cup peas or steamed broccoli
½ cup parmesan cheese
¼ cup fresh basil
⅛ teaspoon cayenne pepper

12 ounces GF spaghetti noodles, cooked

In a large frying pan, sauté the ham, onion, and garlic in the olive oil. Add the remaining ingredients and cook until heated through. Serve over the noodles.

Total carbs 20g - not including noodles

Ham and Cheese Melts *

6 ounces cream cheese, softened
1 teaspoon prepared mustard

¾ cup cheddar cheese, grated
¼ cup Swiss or provolone cheese, grated
¾ cup fully cooked ham, diced
¼ cup chives
¼ teaspoon cayenne

12 slices of GF bread

Preheat the oven to 350° and lightly grease a large cookie sheet. In a medium bowl, mix the cream cheese and mustard until they are well blended. Add the cheeses, ham, chives and cayenne pepper. Mix well. Spread about 2 tablespoons of the cheese mixture on each piece of bread and place on the cookie sheet. Bake for 12-15 minutes.

Carbs from the bread only

Ham with Pear Topping *

1 pound ham steak
1 tablespoon oil

1 – 15 ounce can pear halves
1 tablespoon flour
¼ teaspoon ground ginger
1 teaspoon fresh mint, snipped

Cut the ham into serving sized pieces. Add the oil to a large frying pan. Cook the ham in the oil until heated through and slightly browned on both sides. While the ham is cooking, drain the pears and save the juice. In a medium bowl, combine the juice from the pears, flour and ginger. Remove the ham to a serving platter and keep warm.

Add the pear juice mixture to the pan and cook until thick and bubbly. Add the pears to the mixture and cook until heated through. Place one pear half on each piece of ham, and spoon the sauce evenly over the ham.

Total carbs 50g

Italian Sausage Pasta *

12 ounces GF noodles, cooked

1 tablespoon olive oil
3-4 Italian chicken sausages, sliced
1 cup onion, diced
½ cup red bell pepper, chopped
2 cloves garlic, crushed

1 - 14 ounce can diced tomatoes, undrained
1 tablespoon Italian seasonings
¼ cup parmesan cheese

Cook the noodles according to package directions. In a large skillet, sauté the sausage, onion, bell pepper and garlic in the olive oil. Once the veggies are tender and slightly browned, add the tomatoes, Italian seasonings, cheese and cooked noodles.

Total carbs 310g - including noodles

Macaroni, Ham, and Cheese Salad

8 ounces macaroni, cooked according to package directions, drained and cooled
2 cups ham, cubed
1 cup cheddar cheese, cubed
1 cup celery, thinly sliced
½ cup mayonnaise
½ cup carrot, grated
2 tablespoons vinegar
1 tablespoon onion, grated
1 teaspoon prepared mustard
1 - 8 ounce can tomato sauce

Mix all ingredients in a large bowl. Refrigerate for at least 1 hour before serving.

Total carbs 210g
About 26g per 1 cup serving including noodles

Maple Pork Chops *

1 pound boneless pork chops
1 teaspoon salt
½ teaspoon pepper
2 tablespoons olive oil

Sauce:
1½ cups apple juice
1 tablespoon flour
1 teaspoon prepared mustard
¼ cup maple syrup
1 teaspoon cider vinegar

Hot cooked GF noodles

Sprinkle the pork chops with salt and pepper. In a large skillet, brown the pork chops in the oil. While they're cooking, mix the sauce ingredients in a small bowl. When the pork is cooked through, add the sauce to the pork in the pan and cook until it's thick and bubbly. Serve over hot cooked noodles.

Total carbs 95g

Oven BBQ Ribs

3 pounds pork ribs
Water

16 ounces barbecue sauce
½ cup onion, finely chopped
½ cup brown sugar
¼ cup honey
¼ cup white sugar
1 teaspoon paprika
1 teaspoon chili powder
1 clove garlic, minced
¼ teaspoon celery salt
¼ teaspoon pepper

Cut the ribs apart and place them in a large stock pot. Cover with water and boil over medium heat until they are cooked through, about 20 minutes. Remove the ribs from the water and allow to drain well. While the ribs are cooking, mix together the remaining ingredients in a medium bowl.

Preheat the oven to 350° and line a 9x13 baking pan with foil. Place the ribs in the pan. Baste with the sauce and bake for 30 minutes.

Total carbs 442g - subtract for sauce not used

Pizza

Crust:
1 batch of pizza crust dough (see pages 26-27)

Easy Sauce:
1 can tomato sauce
1 tablespoon Italian seasonings
½ teaspoon salt
½ teaspoon sugar
¼ teaspoon powdered garlic
¼ teaspoon powdered onion

2 tablespoons olive oil

Better Sauce:
¼ cup onion, finely chopped
1 clove garlic, minced
2 teaspoons olive oil
1 - 8 ounce can tomato sauce
1 tablespoon Italian seasonings
½ teaspoon salt
½ teaspoon sugar

Toppings:
2 cups or more mozzarella cheese, grated
Pepperoni *or*
Canadian bacon and pineapple *or*
Browned Italian sausage *or* be creative!

Prepare the pizza crust according to the directions. If using the better sauce, place the onion, garlic, and oil in a small sauce pan. Sauté until tender. Add the remaining ingredients, heat through, and pour over the crust. Otherwise mix the easy sauce ingredients in a small bowl and spread over the crust.

Once the crust is cooked, remove the crust from the pan. Spread the olive oil over the pan and place the empty pan back in the hot oven for 3-4 minutes. Add the cheese and desired toppings to the crust. Return the pizza to the hot pan and bake for 15 to 20 minutes or until the cheese is melted.

Carbs- see crust recipe and add for whatever toppings you put on
Total carbs for the sauce 25g carbs

Pork and Apple Skewers

¾ cup barbecue sauce
¼ cup orange juice
1 tablespoon honey
2 teaspoons prepared mustard
¼ cup brown sugar
2 tablespoons GF soy sauce
1 tablespoon olive oil

1½ pounds pork, cubed

4 medium apples, cut into chunks

In a medium bowl, mix the first 7 ingredients, barbecue sauce through olive oil. Add the pork, mix well and allow to marinate for at least 1 hour. Thread the pork onto skewers alternating with the apple pieces. Baste with the remaining marinade and broil or barbeque for 8-10 minutes.

Total carbs 145g
About 15g carbs per skewer

Potato Bacon Casserole

4 cups frozen hash-browns (shredded or cubed)
½ cup onion, finely chopped
8 ounces bacon, cooked and crumbled
1 cup shredded cheddar cheese
1 - 12 ounce can evaporated milk
1 large egg, lightly beaten
1½ teaspoons seasoned salt

Preheat the oven to 350° and grease 8 inch square baking dish. Layer half the potatoes, half the onion, half the bacon and half the cheese in dish. Repeat the layers. In a small bowl, combine the evaporated milk, egg, and seasoned salt. Pour evenly over the layers in the pan. Cover and bake for 55-60 minutes, uncover and bake additional 5 minutes. Let stand 10-15 minutes before serving.

Total carbs 135g

Potato Lasagna

2 tablespoons olive oil
1 teaspoon garlic powder
1 teaspoon lemon pepper
1 teaspoon salt
½ teaspoon pepper

2 pounds potatoes, sliced ¼ inch thick

8 ounces Italian sausage
½ cup onion, chopped

2 -10 ounce packages of frozen spinach,
    thawed and squeezed dry
1 cup cottage *or* ricotta cheese
2 cups shredded mozzarella cheese

½ cup chicken broth
¼ cup parmesan cheese

Preheat the oven to 350°. Grease a 9x13 pan. Line two cookie sheets with foil and lightly grease. Combine olive oil through pepper in a large bowl. Add the potatoes and toss to coat. Spread the potatoes on the cookie sheets in a single layer and bake for 35-40 minutes.

Meanwhile, brown the sausage in a medium sauce pan. Add the onions and cook until soft.

Layer the 9x13 pan with half of each of the potatoes, sausage mixture, spinach, cottage cheese, and mozzarella cheese. Make a second layer of each. Then pour the chicken broth over the top and sprinkle with the parmesan cheese. Cover with foil and bake for 30-35 minutes.

Total carbs 285g

Potato Sausage Skillet *

1 pound new potatoes, cubed
¼ cup water

4 slices bacon

3 brats, sliced
¾ onion, chopped

2 tablespoons brown sugar
1 tablespoon vinegar
2 teaspoons prepared mustard
½ teaspoon thyme
½ teaspoon pepper
¼ teaspoon cayenne
2 cups fresh baby spinach or kale

½ cup grated parmesan cheese

Place potatoes and water in a microwave save bowl. Cook on high for 3-4 minutes, until potatoes are tender. Drain and set aside.

In a large skillet, cook the bacon. When done, remove and keep warm. Pour out most of the bacon grease. Add the brats and onion to the pan. Cook until the onions are tender and slightly browned. Add the potatoes, crumbled bacon, and remaining ingredients except parmesan cheese. Heat through. Place in a serving bowl, top with the parmesan cheese and serve.

Total carbs 95g

Potato Toppers

6 large baking potatoes

Cheese sauce:
2 tablespoons butter
3 tablespoons flour
2 cups milk
2 cups cheddar cheese, grated
1 teaspoon salt
½ teaspoon pepper

1 package of bacon, cooked
4 cups broccoli flowerets, steamed
Sour cream

Bake the 6 potatoes in the oven or microwave. In a small sauce pan, melt the butter and mix in the flour. Add the milk, whisk until it's smooth, and cook until it's thick and bubbly. Remove from heat. Add the salt, pepper, and cheese and mix until the cheese is melted.

Serve the potatoes topped with the crumbled bacon, cheese sauce, broccoli, and sour cream.

About 40g for each potato
About 5g carbs per ¼ cup cheese sauce
Add for broccoli

Quiche

½ pie crust recipe (see page 154)

1 cup cheddar cheese
½ pound lean pork sausage, cooked
½ cup mushrooms, chopped
½ cup frozen spinach, squeezed dry
2 cups milk
4 eggs
½ teaspoons salt
¼ teaspoon pepper

Preheat the oven to 350° and line a 9 inch pie plate with the pie dough. Spread the cheese in the bottom of the crust, followed by the sausage and spinach. In a medium bowl, beat the milk, eggs, salt, and pepper together and pour over the top. Bake for 35-40 minutes.

Total carbs 125g
About 15g carbs per ⅛ slice

Rice, Beans, and Brats *

1 tablespoon oil
½ cup onion, chopped
¼ cup red bell pepper, chopped
2 cloves garlic, minced
2 Italian spiced chicken sausages, sliced

1 - 15 ounce can kidney beans, drained and rinsed
1 - 15 ounce can black beans, drained and rinsed
1¼ cups chicken broth
3 tablespoons brown sugar
¼ cup ketchup
2 tablespoons molasses
1 tablespoon prepared mustard
1 cup uncooked instant brown rice

Place the oil in a large frying pan. Add the onion, bell pepper, garlic, and sausages. Cook on medium-high heat until the veggies are crisp tender. Add the remaining ingredients and cover tightly. Simmer for 10 minutes or until the rice is tender.

Total carbs 290g
About 37g carbs per 1 cup serving

Sausage and Bean Skillet *

2 teaspoons oil
1 medium onion, sliced
2 cloves garlic, minced
4 brats, sliced

½ cup chicken broth
1 - 15 ounce can diced tomatoes
1 - 15 ounce can baked beans
2 teaspoons Worcestershire sauce
½ teaspoon pepper
¼ teaspoon cayenne pepper

Hot cooked rice or GF noodles

Heat the oil in a large skillet. Sauté the onion, garlic, and brats until slightly browned. Add the remaining ingredients. Cook until heated through. Serve over rice or noodles.

Total carbs 112g – not including rice or noodles

Super Easy Crock Pot Ham

1 medium ham - make sure it fits in the crock pot
½ cup brown sugar.

Grease the crock pot. Place ham in the crock pot. Place the brown sugar on top of the ham and cook on low for 3-4 hours.

Total carbs 110g

Sweet and Sour Pork

Marinade:
1 egg
1 tablespoon sugar
1 tablespoon salt
1 tablespoon GF soy sauce
1 pound cubed pork

Sauce:
3 tablespoons vinegar
3 tablespoons brown sugar
2 tablespoons GF soy sauce
1 tablespoon corn starch
¾ cup reserved pineapple juice

Veggies:
1 onion, cut into wedges
1 green bell pepper, sliced
½ inch ginger, grated
1 clove garlic, minced
1 tomato, cut into wedges
1 can of pineapple chunks, reserve juice

2 tablespoons oil
½ - ¼ cup cornstarch

Hot cooked rice

In a medium bowl, mix all the marinade ingredients and marinate the pork for 30 minutes. Mix the sauce ingredients in a small bowl and cut up veggies. Then in a large frying pan or wok, heat the oil. Dredge the marinated pork in cornstarch. Start with ½ cup and add more as necessary.

Fry the pork in the hot oil until browned. Remove the pork from the pan and keep warm. Add the onion, peppers, ginger, and garlic to the frying pan for 2-3 minutes. Add more oil if needed. Next add the tomato, pineapple, and sauce and cook until it thickens. Add the pork and heat through. Serve over hot cooked rice.

Total carbs 200g - not including rice

Sweet and Sour Meatballs:

Substitute **1 pound ground beef** for the pork and marinade. In a medium bowl, add ½ **cup chopped onion, 1 teaspoon salt** and ½ **teaspoon pepper** to the beef. Mix well. Form into 1 inch meatballs and fry in 1 tablespoon oil over medium-high heat until cooked through and browned on all sides.

Tangy BBQ Pork
(Amazingly delicious!)

8 boneless pork chops
¼ cup Worcestershire sauce
¼ cup GF soy sauce
1 tablespoon garlic powder
1 tablespoon onion powder
½ tablespoon salt
½ tablespoon pepper
¼ cup barbeque sauce
1 teaspoon crushed red pepper flakes
3 tablespoons ketchup

Mix all ingredients together and marinate for at least 1 hour. Barbeque, flipping once, until done. About 10-15 minutes depending on the thickness of the pork chops.

Total carbs 80g

Southwest Pork *

Pork:
1 tablespoon oil
1 pound pork, cubed
1 teaspoon salt
½ teaspoon pepper

1½ cups fresh salsa

Hot cooked rice
1 avocado, cubed
Sour Cream

Fresh Salsa:
3 cups tomatoes, chopped
½ cup onion, finely chopped
½ cup bell pepper, chopped
3 tablespoons lime juice
2 tablespoons fresh parsley, chopped
3 cloves garlic, minced
1 jalapeño, finely chopped, *or*
    cayenne pepper to taste
½ teaspoon salt

Season the pork with salt and pepper. In a large skillet, sauté the pork in the oil. Cook until done and browned on both sides. In a medium bowl, mix all the fresh salsa ingredients, or use store-bought fresh salsa. Add the salsa to the pork and bring to a boil. Simmer for 5 minutes or until sauce has thickened a little. Serve the pork over rice, topped with avocado and sour cream.

Total carbs 40g - not including rice

Notes:

Soups, Stews,
and Sauces

Any recipe with an * is one that can be made in about 30 minutes

African Chicken Soup

1 tablespoon oil
1½ cups sweet potato, cubed
½ cup red bell pepper, chopped
½ cup onion, chopped
2 cloves garlic, minced

3 cups water
2 cups chicken broth
½ pound chicken tenders
1 cup salsa
⅓ cup uncooked rice

1 -15 ounce can black beans, drained and rinsed
⅓ cup peanut butter

In a large stock pot, sauté the veggies in the oil until they are tender, sweet potatoes through garlic. Potatoes may not be fully cooked. Add the water, broth, and the chicken and cook until the chicken is done. Remove the chicken and shred. Add the chicken back to the pot along with all the remaining ingredients. Simmer for 1 hour or until the rice is cooked.

Total carbs 205g
About 25 per 1 cup serving

Basic Beef Stew

1 tablespoon oil
1 pound beef, cubed
1 beef bone (optional)
1 cup onion, chopped
3 stalks celery, chopped
4 cups water
4-5 carrots, chopped

3 potatoes, peeled and chopped
½ cup tapioca
2 bay leaves
1 teaspoon sugar
1 - 8 ounce can tomato sauce
2 teaspoons salt
1 teaspoon pepper

Brown the beef in the oil and then add the onion and celery. Cook until the veggies are tender. Add the remaining ingredients and simmer for at least 2 hours. 6-8 hours in a crock pot on low is even better.

Total carbs 245g
About 30g carbs per 1 cup serving

Black Bean Soup *

1 tablespoon olive oil
1 onion, finely chopped
2 cloves garlic, crushed
2 stalks celery, finely chopped
½ cup red bell pepper, finely chopped

2 cups chicken broth
1 - 15 ounce can black beans, drained and rinsed
1 teaspoon salt
1 teaspoon cumin
2 tablespoons lemon juice
1 cup cooked chicken, shredded

Sour cream

In a large pot, sauté the onion, garlic, celery, and bell pepper in the olive oil until tender. Add the remaining ingredients except sour cream and heat through. (If you don't have cooked chicken, sauté 2 chicken tenders along with the veggies.) Serve with a dollop of sour cream.

Total carbs 155g
About 55g carbs per 1 cup serving

"Canned" Tomato Soup *

(In case you're craving that childhood taste to go with your grilled cheese sandwich)

1 - 12 ounce can tomato paste
5 cups water
½ teaspoon garlic salt
1½ teaspoons salt
3 tablespoons sugar
1 cup milk (or additional water)

In a medium pan, mix all the ingredients except milk and bring almost to a boil. Remove from heat and add the milk. (If it's too hot, the milk will curdle).

Total carbs 77g
About 12g carbs per 1 cup serving

Cannellini Bean and Sausage Stew

1 tablespoon olive oil
2 pounds kielbasa sausage
1 cup onion, diced
3 stalks celery, diced
2 red bell peppers, diced
3 cloves garlic, minced
Red pepper flakes to taste

2 cups chicken broth
3 cups water
2 tablespoons parsley
1 bay leaf
1 fresh thyme sprig

1 fresh rosemary sprig
1 fresh sage sprig
2 - 15 ounce cans cannellini beans
1 - 15 ounce can petite diced tomatoes
½ cup uncooked rice

2 cups baby spinach

Crumb Topping
2 cups fresh GF bread crumbs
2 tablespoons butter
1 teaspoon salt
½ teaspoon pepper

In a medium frying pan, sauté the sausage, onion, celery, and peppers in the oil until the veggies are tender and the sausage is slightly browned. Add the garlic and red pepper flakes and cook 1 minute more. Place the veggies and sausage in a crock pot along with all other ingredients except the spinach. Cook on low for 3-4 hours. Fold in the spinach.

In a small bowl, mix the crumb topping ingredients. Sauté in a small frying pan until the crumbs are browned. Serve stew with crumbs sprinkled on top.

Total carbs 280g
About 35g carbs per 1 cup serving

Chicken Noodle Soup

(Comfort food at its best)

1 tablespoon oil
1 cup onions, chopped
1½ cups celery, chopped
1½ cups carrots, chopped
4 cups chicken broth
½ pound chicken tenders

1 tablespoon parsley
1 bay leaf
2 teaspoons salt
1 teaspoon pepper

4 ounces uncooked GF fettuccini noodles

In a large stock pot, sauté the onions, carrots, and celery in the oil. Add the broth and chicken, and cook over medium heat until the chicken is cooked. Remove the chicken and shred it, then add it back to the pot with the remaining ingredients except the noodles. Simmer for at least 2 hours.

About 20 minutes before serving, break the noodles into 2 inch pieces, add the noodles and cook 20 minutes or until they're done.

Total carbs 80g - About 10g carbs per 1 cup serving

❖ *Chicken and Rice Soup*:

Leave out the noodles and add **1 cup cooked rice** about 10 minutes before serving.

Total carbs 80g - About 10g carbs per 1 cup serving

❖ *Chicken and Dumpling Soup*:

Mix **2 eggs**, **1 tablespoon milk**, and ½ **teaspoon salt** in a small bowl. Add enough **flour** to make a thick paste about 1½ cups. Add the paste 1 teaspoon at a time to the boiling soup. Cook for 10 minutes longer.

Total carbs 170g - About 5g carbs per 1 cup serving, plus 5g carbs per dumpling

Chicken Tortilla Soup *

1 tablespoon olive oil
½ cup onion, chopped
1 clove garlic, minced

4 cups water
1 pound chicken tenders

½ teaspoon cumin
1 – 28 ounce can crushed tomatoes
½ cup salsa
1 tablespoon parsley
2 teaspoons oregano

Shredded cheddar cheese
Tortilla chips

In a large pot, sauté the onions and garlic in olive oil. Add the water and chicken and cook over medium heat until the chicken is cooked. Remove the chicken, shred it, and return it to the pot. Add the remaining ingredients except cheese and chips, and cook until heated through. Serve with shredded cheese and tortilla chips.

Total carbs 116g
About 15g carbs per 1 cup serving, not including tortilla chips

Chili Soup *

1 pound ground beef
1 cup onion, chopped
2 cloves garlic, minced

1 - 28 ounce can crushed tomatoes
2 - 15 ounce cans red kidney beans, drained and rinsed
1 tablespoon chili powder
1 teaspoon oregano
1 teaspoon cumin
1 teaspoon salt
¼ teaspoon cayenne pepper

Shredded cheddar cheese

In a large pot, brown the beef. Add the onion and garlic and cook until tender. Add the remaining ingredients and simmer for 15-20 minutes. Serve with shredded cheese on top.

Total carbs 230g
About 28g carbs per 1 cup serving

Corn Chowder *

4 slices bacon

2 tablespoons butter
1 cup onion, chopped
1 cup celery, chopped
1 clove garlic, minced

¼ cup flour

3 cups milk
2 cups chicken broth
2 cups potatoes, cubed
1½ cups corn
1 cup cooked chicken, shredded
1 teaspoon thyme
1 teaspoon parsley
1 bay leaf
1 teaspoon salt
½ teaspoon pepper

In a large pot, cook the bacon until done. Set aside. Add the butter, onion, celery, and garlic to the pan with the bacon drippings. Cook until tender. Add the flour and mix well. Stir in the remaining ingredients. Cook over medium heat, stirring frequently, until thick and bubbly and the potatoes are cooked, 15-20 minutes.

Total carbs 180g
About 20g carbs per 1 cup serving

Creamy Chicken and Broccoli Soup *

¼ cup butter
¼ cup onion
½ cup mushrooms
½ cup carrots
1½ cups broccoli flowerets

¼ cup flour

3 cups milk
1 cup chicken broth

1 cup cooked chicken, shredded
1½ cups cooked brown rice
½ teaspoon basil
1 tablespoon Worcestershire sauce
1 teaspoon salt
½ teaspoon pepper
1 cup cooked brown rice

1 cup grated cheddar cheese

In a large stock pot, sauté the veggies in the butter until crisp tender. Add the flour, mix well and then add the milk and broth. Cook until thick and bubbly. Add the chicken into the pot along with all the remaining ingredients, except the cheese. Add cheese to right before serving.

Total carbs 80g
About 10g carbs per 1 cup serving

Ham and Bean Soup

1 tablespoon olive oil
1 cup onion, chopped
1 cup celery, chopped
2 cloves of garlic, minced

5 cups water
1 ham hock with some meat remaining
1 cup carrots, chopped
1 teaspoon oregano
2 tablespoons red wine vinegar

1 teaspoon salt
½ teaspoon pepper
1 - 20 ounce can crushed tomatoes

1 cup lentils
2 - 16 ounce cans red beans,
    drained and rinsed
1 - 16 ounce can black beans,
    drained and rinsed

In a large pot, sauté the onions, celery, and garlic in the olive oil. Add the next 8 ingredients, ham through tomatoes. Simmer for 2 hours or more. Remove the bone and cut off any meat. Cut the meat into bites sized pieces and return them to the pan. Add the lentils and beans, and cook for another hour.

Total carbs 380g
About 30g carbs per 1 cup serving

Ham and Split Pea Soup

1 pound dried split peas, washed
4 cups water
4 cups chicken broth

1 ham hock with some meat remaining
2 teaspoons salt
2 teaspoons black pepper
1 bay leaf
2 teaspoons fresh thyme

3 tablespoons butter
1 cup onions, finely chopped
½ cup celery, finely chopped
1 cup carrots, chopped
2 cloves garlic, minced

Place the washed peas in a large pot and cover with the water and chicken broth. Bring to a boil. Add the ham hock, salt, pepper, bay leaf, and thyme and simmer for 30 minutes.

In a small pot, melt the butter over medium-high heat. Add the onions, celery and carrots. Cook until tender, 3-5 minutes. Add the garlic and cook, for one minute more. Add the veggies to the pot and simmer for 40 minutes.

Remove the ham hock and bay leaf. Cut the meat off the bone and set aside. Discard the bone. With a hand held blender, puree the peas and veggies. Add the ham back in, heat through, and serve.

Total carbs 280g
About 24g carbs per 1 cup serving

Homemade Tomato Soup *

1 tablespoon olive oil
½ cup onion, chopped
½ cup celery, chopped

2 – 28 ounce cans tomato sauce
2 teaspoons chicken bouillon
1 tablespoon parsley
1 tablespoon sugar
¼ teaspoon cayenne pepper

In a stock pot, sauté the onions and celery in the olive oil. Add one can of the tomato sauce and puree in a blender until smooth. Return the mixture to the pot and add the other can of tomato sauce along with the remaining ingredients. Cook until heated through.

Total carbs 104g
About 34g carbs per 1 cup serving

Mulligatawny Stew

(This is a large recipe)

6 tablespoons butter
2 cups onion, chopped
2 cups carrots, chopped
1 cup celery, chopped
1 cup red pepper, chopped
9 cloves garlic, minced
2 potatoes, peeled and cubed

½ teaspoon cayenne
5 tablespoons curry powder
1 teaspoon turmeric
½ cup flour

7 cups chicken broth
2 cups milk
2 cups cream

4 cups chicken, cooked and shredded
3 apples, peeled and diced
1 – 14 ounce can coconut milk

2 cups cooked rice

In a large pot, sauté the veggies, onion through potatoes, in the butter until tender. In a small bowl, mix together the spices and flour and add to the veggies. In a large bowl, mix together the broth, milk and cream. Add the liquid slowly, stirring well. Then add the chicken, apples, and coconut milk and simmer for 1 hour. Just before serving add the rice and heat through.

Total carbs 328g
About 15g carbs per 1 cup serving

Moroccan Tomato Soup

(Or Christmas Tomato Soup)

1 tablespoon olive oil
1 cup onion, coarsely chopped
2 cloves garlic, minced
2 - 28 ounce cans crushed tomatoes
1½ cups chicken broth
1 cup orange juice
3 tablespoons honey

1 cinnamon stick
1 teaspoon allspice
¼ teaspoon cinnamon
¼ teaspoon nutmeg
2 large potatoes cut into ¼-½ inch cubes
1 teaspoon salt
½ teaspoon pepper

In a large stock pot, sauté the onions and garlic until tender. Place in a blender and add some of the crushed tomatoes. Blend just until smooth. Return the mixture to the pot. Add the remaining ingredients and simmer on medium-low heat for 1 hour or until the potatoes are done. Garnish with fresh mint leaves if desired.

Total carbs 248g
About 41g carbs per 1 cup serving

Nacho Cheese Soup *

½ pound ground beef
1 tablespoon olive oil
½ cup onions, chopped

¼ cup flour
3 cups milk

¾ cup salsa
½ cup corn

2 tablespoons green chilies
1 tablespoon taco seasoning
¾ teaspoon salt
¼ teaspoon pepper
¼ teaspoon cayenne pepper
3 cups grated cheddar cheese

Tortilla chips
Sour cream

In a large pot, brown the ground beef in the olive oil. Add the onions and cook until tender. Mix the flour in with the meat, add the milk and stir well. Mix in the remaining ingredients. Bring to a boil, stirring frequently. Serve with chips for dipping and a dollop of sour cream.

Total carbs 58g
About 8g carbs per 1 cup serving

Pepperoni Soup *

1 tablespoon oil
1 pound ground beef
1 cup sliced pepperoni, cut in half
½ cup onion
½ cup green or red bell pepper, chopped
¼ cup mushrooms
2 cloves garlic, minced

2 cups chicken broth
2 cups water
1 – 28 ounce can crushed tomatoes
1 tablespoon Italian seasonings
1 teaspoon salt
½ teaspoon pepper

Brown the beef in a large stock pot in the oil. Add the pepperoni and veggies, and cook until they are tender. Add the remaining ingredients and simmer for 10 minutes.

Total carbs 100g
About 12g carbs per 1 cup serving

Potato Soup with Bacon *

6 potatoes, cubed
4 cups water

⅓ cup butter
¼ cup onion, chopped
⅓ cup flour
4 cups milk
¼ teaspoon dill weed
½ cup cheddar cheese, shredded
1 teaspoon salt
½ teaspoon pepper

Shredded cheddar cheese
1 pound bacon, cooked and crumbled

Place the potatoes and water in a large pot. Boil the potatoes until they are soft and then drain, reserving 1 cup of the cooking water. In a large mixing bowl, coarsely mash the potatoes with the reserved cooking water so that some bite-sized chunks remain. (A large wire whisk works well.)

In the now empty pot, sauté the onions in the butter until they are soft. Mix in the flour, and then add the milk, and stir well. Add the remaining ingredients including the potatoes. Heat until thick and bubbly, stirring frequently. Serve with additional shredded cheese and crumbled bacon.

Total carbs 300g
About 38g carbs per 1 cup serving

Potato Swiss Chowder *

1 tablespoon olive oil
1 cup onion, chopped
1 clove garlic, minced

1 cup chicken broth
3 cups milk
2 large potatoes, cubed
1 cup sweet potato, cubed

½ cup cooked brown or wild rice
½ cup shredded Swiss cheese
2 bay leaves
1 teaspoon parsley
1 teaspoon salt
½ teaspoon pepper

In a large stock pot, sauté the onion and garlic until tender. Add the chicken broth, milk, and both types of potatoes. Simmer for 15-20 minutes or until the potatoes are cooked. Place ½ of the soup base in the blender and puree until smooth. Return it to the remainder of the soup and add the rice, cheese, and seasonings. Simmer for 10 minutes and serve.

Total carbs 100g
About 23g carbs per 1 cup serving

Refried Bean Soup*

1 tablespoon oil
½ cup onion, chopped
1 clove garlic, minced

1 -28 ounce can crushed tomatoes
1 - 31 ounce can refried beans
2 cups chicken broth
1 tablespoon parsley

1 tablespoon chili powder
½ teaspoon cayenne pepper
1 teaspoon sugar

1½ cups shredded cheddar cheese
⅓ cup sour cream

Tortilla chips

In a large pot, sauté the onion and garlic in the oil until tender. Add the next 7 ingredients, tomatoes through sugar. Bring to a boil, stirring frequently. Remove from heat and add the cheese and sour cream. Serve with tortilla chips.

Total carbs 174g
About 22g carbs per 1 cup serving - without tortilla chips

Sweet Potato and Black Bean Soup*

2 tablespoons olive oil
1 medium sweet potato, peeled and diced
1 cup onion, diced

3 cloves garlic, minced
2 tablespoons chili powder
4 teaspoons cumin
½ teaspoon cayenne pepper
½ teaspoon salt

2½ cups water
1 - 15 ounce can black beans, drained and rinsed
1 - 14 ounce can petite diced tomatoes
4 teaspoons lime juice

¼ cup fresh cilantro, chopped

In a large pot, sauté the sweet potatoes and onion in the olive oil until the onion is tender. The potato will not be fully cooked. Add the garlic and spices, chili through salt, and cook 1 minute more. Add all remaining ingredients except cilantro, and simmer for 15 -20 minutes or until the sweet potato is cooked. Add cilantro and serve.

Total carbs 220g
About 25g per 1 cup serving

Taco Soup*

1 pound ground beef
1 cup onion, chopped
2 cloves garlic, minced

1½ cups water
1 – 28 ounce can crushed tomatoes
1 – 16 ounce can kidney beans
1 – 16 ounce can black beans
½ cup ranch dressing

1 jalapeño pepper, diced
1 - 16 ounce can corn
1 packet taco seasoning
1 teaspoon salt

Toppings:
Sour cream
Cheddar cheese, grated
Tortilla chips, crushed

In a large pot, brown the ground beef. Add the onions and garlic, and cook until tender. Add the remaining ingredients except the toppings. Allow to simmer for 15-20 minutes. Serve with a dollop of sour cream, a sprinkle of cheese and crushed tortilla chips.

Total carbs 281g – not including chips
About 25g carbs per 1 cup serving plus chips

White Chicken Chili

1 tablespoon oil
2 fire roasted chilies
2 bell peppers, diced
1 small onion diced
3 cloves garlic, minced

1 bunch cilantro, chopped
3 cups chicken, cooked and shredded
1 tablespoon cumin
1 teaspoon salt
½ teaspoon garlic salt

1 - 15 ounce can white kidney beans
1 - 15 ounce can hominy
1 - 15 ounce can petite diced tomatoes
4 cups chicken broth
1 tablespoon lime juice

Toppings:
Tortilla chips
Shredded cheese
Sour cream
2 limes, quartered

In a large pan, sauté the chilies, bell peppers, onions, and garlic in the oil. Once they are tender, add to the crock pot with the remaining ingredients. Cook on high for 2-3 hours or on low for 6-8 hours. Serve with tortilla chips, shredded cheese, sour cream and limes.

Total carbs 145g – not including chips or toppings
About 13g carbs per 1 cup serving

-Sauces-

Basic White Sauce

1 tablespoon butter
1 tablespoon flour
1 cup milk
Dash of salt

Melt the butter in a medium sauce pan over medium-high heat. Mix in the flour. Add the milk and salt, and whisk the mixture until blended. Cook, stirring frequently, until it's thick and bubbly.

This can be used as the base for any kind of cheese sauce.

Total carbs 20g

Cream Soup Base

(This can be used in casserole recipes in place of one can of cream soup. Just add the mushrooms, potatoes or whatever will make it the type of cream soup the recipe needs.)

2 tablespoons butter
1 teaspoon onion powder
2 tablespoons flour
1 teaspoon salt
¼ teaspoon pepper
⅛ teaspoon cayenne pepper
1 cup milk
¾ cup chicken or vegetable broth

In a large sauce pan, melt the butter. Add the flour and mix well. Then add the remaining ingredients. Cook, stirring frequently, until it forms a thick sauce.

Total carbs 25g
Add carbs for additional ingredients

Cheese Sauce

1 tablespoon butter
1 tablespoon flour
1 cup milk
1 teaspoon salt
¼ teaspoon pepper
2 cups shredded cheddar cheese, or
      1 cup parmesan cheese

Melt the butter in a medium sauce pan over medium-high heat. Mix in the flour. Add the milk and salt, and whisk the mixture until blended. Cook, stirring frequently, until it's thick and bubbly.
Add the cheese and stir until melted and well mixed.

Total carbs 20g

Notes:

Notes:

Meatless Main Dishes

Any recipe with an * is one that can be made in about 30 minutes

Black Bean Pie

4 GF tortillas (see page 21)

1 tablespoon olive oil
½ cup onion, chopped
2 cloves garlic, minced
½ teaspoon cumin
½ teaspoon cayenne pepper
1 teaspoon salt
½ teaspoon black pepper

2 – 15 ounce cans black beans,
    drained and rinsed
1 bottle GF beer
2 cups corn
4 green onions, chopped

2½ cups cheddar cheese, grated
Sour cream

Preheat the oven to 350°. Grease a round casserole dish big enough for the tortillas to fit and set aside. In a medium frying pan, heat the olive oil. Add the onion and spices, garlic through pepper. Cook until the onions are tender. Add the beans, beer, and corn, and simmer until the liquid is almost gone.

Remove from the heat and add the green onions. Place the first tortilla in the bottom of the casserole dish. Layer ¼ of the bean mixture and ½ cup of the cheese. Repeat this with the rest of the tortillas and spread the remaining cheese on top. Bake for 25 minutes. Serve with sour cream.

Total carbs 335g
About 42g carbs per ⅛ wedge serving

Cheese Fondue *

1 clove garlic, cut in half
4 cups cheddar cheese, grated (about 1 pound)
¼ cup milk
¼ cup white wine
1 teaspoon prepared mustard
1 egg yolk

GF French bread, cubed
Apples, cubed
Steamed broccoli flowerets

Rub the inside of the fondue pot or medium sauce pan with the garlic clove. Heat the milk and wine over low heat. Add the cheese and let it melt. Stir in the mustard and egg yolk and cook until thick and creamy. Serve in the center of the table to allow everyone to dip the bread, apples, and broccoli in the cheese sauce.

Total carbs 6g for the cheese sauce
Add carbs for bread, apples, and broccoli

Italian Lost Toast *

Tomato sauce:
2 tablespoons onion, finely chopped
1 clove garlic, minced
1 tablespoon olive oil

1 - 28 ounce can crushed tomatoes
2 tablespoons sugar
2 teaspoons balsamic vinegar
1 teaspoon salt
½ teaspoon pepper

Toast:
1 tablespoon olive oil
¼ parmesan cheese, grated
1½ cups milk
1 tablespoon flour
3 eggs
⅛ teaspoon nutmeg

1¾ cups shredded parmesan cheese
6 slices GF bread

6 eggs
1 tablespoon oil

In a medium sauce pan, sauté the onion and garlic in the oil until tender. Stir in the remaining tomato sauce ingredients. Allow to simmer for about 20 minutes.

For the toast, heat the oil in a large skillet over medium-high heat. In a large shallow bowl, mix the parmesan cheese, milk, flour, eggs, and nutmeg. Put the remaining parmesan cheese in a separate, medium, shallow bowl.

Soak the bread in the egg mixture and then press into the shredded cheese. Place the bread in the skillet and cook, flipping once until both sides are golden, about 5-6 minutes. Do several batches if needed. In another large skillet, fry six eggs in the remaining tablespoon of oil. Serve the toast covered with tomato sauce and topped with a fried egg.

Total carbs for the tomato sauce 60g
Plus carbs for the bread

Macaroni and Cheese *

3 tablespoons butter
3 tablespoons onion, finely chopped
4 tablespoons flour
2 cups milk
1 tablespoon white wine
1 teaspoon salt
½ teaspoon pepper
2 cups shredded cheddar cheese
¼ teaspoon prepared mustard

12 ounces GF noodles, cooked and drained

Cook the noodle according to the package directions. Grease a 9x9 pan or casserole dish of equivalent size.

Preheat the oven to broil. In a medium pan, melt the butter and then add the onion. Cook until the onion is tender. Add the flour and mix well. Next add the milk and whisk until it's smooth. Cook, stirring frequently, until it's thick and bubbly. Add the wine, salt, pepper, cheese, and mustard. Mix well. Pour over the cooked, drained noodles and place in the pan or a casserole dish. Place under the broiler for 5 minutes until the top is crisp and browned.

Total carbs 300g - including noodles
About 23g carbs per ½ cup serving

Spinach-Stuffed Shells

1 box of GF jumbo shells
2 – 10 ounce packages frozen spinach,
    thawed and squeezed dry
1½ cups ricotta or cottage cheese
2 tablespoons fresh oregano, chopped
2 cloves garlic, minced

3 tablespoons flour
3 cups milk
½ teaspoon salt
¼ teaspoon nutmeg
1½ cups shredded mozzarella cheese
½ cup shredded Swiss cheese

3 tablespoons butter

Preheat the oven to 350° and grease a 9x13 pan. Cook the shells according to package directions. While they cook, mix the spinach, ricotta or cottage cheese, oregano, and garlic powder in a medium bowl and set aside. In a medium sauce pan, melt the butter, add the flour to the melted butter and stir well. Add the milk. Stir until smooth and cook over medium heat until it thickens. Add the salt, nutmeg, and remaining cheeses. Remove from the heat and stir until the cheeses are melted.

Drain the shells and arrange them in the prepared pan. Spoon spinach mixture into each shell until they are all filled. Pour the hot cheese sauce over the top. Cover with foil and bake for 20-25 minutes.

Total carbs 240g
About 7g carbs per shell

Tip:
If you can't find GF shells, use GF lasagna noodles. Cook according to package directions. Lay out the noodles and spread the spinach mixture along each one, covering the noodle. Roll up the noodles. Place them in a 9x9 pan and pour the cheese sauce over the top. Cover and bake for 20-15 minutes.

Vegetable Lasagna

3 tablespoons butter
½ cup onions, chopped
2 cloves garlic, minced
1 cup carrots, julienned
1 cup broccoli flowerets, cut small
1 zucchini, julienned
1 cup tomatoes, chopped
1 cup baby spinach leaves
½ cup mushrooms, sliced

1 tablespoon Italian seasonings
1 teaspoon salt
3 tablespoons flour
2 cups milk
2 cups shredded mozzarella cheese
2 cups ricotta cheese

½ cup grated parmesan cheese
1 package GF lasagna noodles

Preheat the oven to 350° and grease a 9x13 pan. Cook the noodles according to the package directions. In the meantime, in a large frying pan, sauté the onions, garlic, and carrots for 5 minutes in the butter. Add the broccoli, zucchini, tomatoes, spinach, and mushrooms and sauté for 5 minutes longer until all the veggies are soft.

Add the Italian seasonings and salt. Mix in the flour and then add the milk. Cook, stirring frequently, until thick and bubbly. Add in the mozzarella and ricotta cheese.

In the pan, layer the noodles and the veggie-cheese sauce in three layers. Sprinkle the top with the parmesan cheese and cover with foil. Bake for 30-40 minutes.

Total carbs 240g
About 20g carbs per 3 inch square

Side Dishes

Avocado Basil Pasta

8 ounces GF noodles

2 medium avocados, coarsely chopped
6 slices of bacon, cooked and crumbled
⅔ cup fresh basil, coarsely chopped
2 tablespoons lemon juice
1 tablespoon olive oil
3 cloves garlic, minced
¼ teaspoon pepper
¼ teaspoon salt

½ cup parmesan cheese, shredded.

Cook the noodles according to the package directions. In a large bowl, mix the remaining ingredients except the cheese. Drain the noodles when they are done. Add the avocado mixture to the hot noodles and top with the cheese. Serve warm.

Total carbs 200g

Baked Red Peppers with Cherry Tomatoes

2 red bell peppers, cut in half lengthwise (stem to end)
1 heaping cup cherry tomatoes
2 ounces feta cheese
1 teaspoon thyme
½ cup fresh basil leaves, chopped
½ teaspoon pepper
1 tablespoon olive oil.

Preheat the oven to 400°. Grease a 9x9 pan. Cut the bell peppers and poke a few holes in the bottom of each half to let juices run out. Place the pepper halves in the pan. In a medium bowl, mix the tomatoes with the remaining ingredients. Fill the peppers with the mixture. Cover the stuffed peppers with foil and bake for 30 minutes. Uncover and bake 15 minutes longer.

Total carbs 40g
About 10g carbs per half

Buttery Garlic Bread

Topping:
¼ cup butter, softened
½ cup parmesan or Romano cheese
¼ cup parsley
2 cloves garlic, minced

1 loaf of GF French bread *or* 10 slices GF sandwich bread

Preheat the oven to 500°. Mix the topping ingredients. Cut the loaf of bread in half lengthwise and spread butter mixture over the two halves. Or spread the topping evenly over the sandwich bread. Place the bread on a cookie sheet and bake for about 5 minutes.

Total carbs depends on the bread
The topping has no carbs

Crock Pot Sweet Potatoes with Applesauce

6 medium sweet potatoes (about 2 pounds)
1½ cups applesauce
⅔ cup brown sugar
3 tablespoons butter, melted
1 teaspoon cinnamon

½ cup walnuts or pecans, toasted and chopped

Cut sweet potatoes into 1 inch cubes. Place in a crock pot with all the remaining ingredients except nuts. Mix well. Cook on low for 4-6 hours. Scoop into a serving bowl and sprinkle with nuts.

Total carbs 300g

Cornbread Stuffing

¼ cup butter
½ cup onion, chopped
2 stalks celery, chopped
2 cloves garlic, minced
1 teaspoon Italian seasonings
1 teaspoon salt
½ teaspoon pepper
⅛ teaspoon cayenne pepper
1½ cups chicken broth
3 cups cornbread, cubed
2 cups GF bread, cubed

Preheat the oven to 350°. Grease a 9x9 pan. In a large sauce pan, sauté the onion and celery in the butter until tender. Add the garlic and cook 1 minute longer. Add the Italian seasonings, salt, pepper, cayenne pepper, and chicken broth, and bring to a boil. Place the cornbread and bread cubes the pan and mix. Pour the broth mixture over the bread crumbs and mix gently until blended. Cover with foil and bake for 20-25 minutes.

Total carbs 200g

Creamy Grilled Corn

6 ears corn, husked

1 tablespoon butter
1 tablespoon flour
½ cup milk
2 ounces cream cheese
1 teaspoon salt
½ teaspoon pepper
Sprinkle of cayenne pepper

Grill the husked corn until cooked and slightly burnt. In a medium sauce pan, melt the butter, add the flour, and mix well. Add the milk and cook until thick and bubbly, stirring frequently. Add the cream cheese, salt, pepper, and cayenne and mix well. Cut the kernels off the cobs and add to the sauce. Serve warm.

Total carbs 230g

Flavorful Jasmine Rice

3 tablespoons oil
⅓ cup fresh ginger, grated
2 cloves garlic, minced
2 cups jasmine rice
2 cups chicken broth
2 cups water
¾ teaspoon salt
1 tablespoon cilantro

In a large sauce pan, cook the ginger and garlic in the oil for 1 minute. Add the remaining ingredients and bring to a boil. Lower the heat and simmer for 18-20 minutes or until the rice is done.

Total carbs 320g

Greek Dinner Salad

Dressing:
¼ cup fresh parsley
3 tablespoons fresh dill
1 tablespoon olive oil
1 tablespoon lemon juice
1 teaspoon oregano

Salad:
6 cups romaine lettuce, chopped
3 tomatoes, chopped
½ cup onion, thinly sliced
¾ cup feta cheese
1 tablespoon capers
1 cucumber, peeled and chopped
1 - 19 ounce can chickpeas, drained and rinsed

In a medium bowl, whisk all dressing ingredients together. In a large bowl, mix the lettuce with the remaining salad ingredients and pour the dressing over the salad. Serve with Greek or Italian food.

Carbs - About 5g carbs per 1 cup serving

Greek Pasta Salad

14 ounces GF shell noodles, uncooked
1 cup mayonnaise
1 cup Italian salad dressing
3 stalks celery, chopped
¼ cup onion, chopped
½ cup black olives, sliced
8 ounces feta cheese
1 teaspoon salt
½ teaspoon pepper
1 tablespoon oregano
1½ cups cherry tomatoes, cut in half

Cook the noodles according to the package directions. Drain, rinse, and cool. Mix the remaining ingredients together in a large bowl and add the noodles. Mix well. Keep in the fridge until ready to serve.

Total carbs 360g

Greek Rice

1 cup white rice
2 cups chicken broth
1 tablespoon butter
1 tablespoon fresh mint leaves
1 tablespoon lemon juice
1 clove garlic, minced

Combine all ingredients in a medium sauce pan. Bring to a boil, then reduce the heat to low and simmer for 18-20 minutes or until the rice is cooked.

Total carbs 160g

Honey Roasted Potatoes

1½ pounds small red *or* golden potatoes, scrubbed
3 tablespoons onion, diced
3 tablespoons butter, melted
2 tablespoons honey
1 teaspoon mustard
1 teaspoon salt
½ teaspoon pepper

Preheat the oven to 375° and line a 9x13 pan with foil. Lightly grease the foil. Cut the unpeeled potatoes into 1 inch cubes. Place them in the prepared pan and cover with the onions. Combine the butter, honey, and mustard, and drizzle over the potatoes. Sprinkle with salt and pepper, and bake for 35-40 minutes, stirring once.

Total carbs 150g

Mediterranean Cucumber Salad

1 large cucumber, coarsely chopped
½ cup plain yogurt
1 teaspoon sugar
1 teaspoon mint

Mix all ingredients and serve with Mediterranean food.

Total carbs 20g
About 5g carbs per ½ cup serving

Moroccan Rice

1 cup white rice
1½ cups chicken broth
2 tablespoons olive oil
½ cup onion, chopped
⅔ cup slivered almonds
½ cup pine nuts
½ teaspoon cumin
¼ teaspoon turmeric

¼ teaspoon cinnamon
¼ teaspoon chili powder
¼ cup raisins
¾ cup orange juice
¼ cup fresh parsley, chopped
½ teaspoon salt
¼ teaspoon pepper

Add all ingredients to a medium sauce pan. Bring to a boil. Reduce the heat to low and simmer for 18-20 minutes or until the rice is cooked.

Total carbs 210g

Orange Cilantro Black Bean Salad

1 teaspoon olive oil
½ medium red onion, cut into wedges
2 cloves garlic, minced
¼ teaspoon ground cumin
1 - 15 ounce can black beans, rinsed and drained
2 tablespoons cilantro, chopped
2 teaspoons red wine vinegar
2 medium oranges, peeled and segments chopped in half
⅛ teaspoon salt
⅛ teaspoon black pepper

In a large skillet, sauté the onion in the oil for 2 minutes. Add the garlic and cumin and cook 1 minute more. Stir in black beans and cook just until heated through. Transfer the bean mixture to a bowl, stir in remaining ingredients and serve.

Total carbs 110g

Oven Fries

4 medium white potatoes
3 tablespoons olive oil
2 tablespoons parmesan cheese, grated
1 teaspoon garlic salt
½ teaspoon pepper

Preheat the oven to 400° and line a cookie sheet with foil. Grease the foil. Peel the potatoes and cut into long, thick slices, about ¼-½ inches thick. Mix the remaining ingredients in a large bowl and add the potatoes, stirring to mix. Spread the potatoes out on the cookie sheet and bake for about 40 minutes, or until golden and soft.

Total carbs 150g

Potato Salad

1 pound medium red potatoes
Water
¼ cup fresh parsley, chopped
¼ cup green onions, chopped
3 hard-boiled eggs, chopped
¼ cup bell pepper, chopped
1 teaspoon lemon pepper
1 teaspoon seasoning salt
1 tablespoon Dijon mustard
¼ cup mayonnaise
1 cup sour cream

Peel the potatoes and cut into 1 inch cubes. In a medium sauce pan, cover the potatoes with water and boil until tender, 8-10 minutes. Drain the potatoes and let them cool. In a large bowl, mix the remaining ingredients. Add the potatoes and chill for several hours before serving.

Total carbs 100g

Rice Bowl Black Beans

2 tablespoons olive oil
1 green bell pepper, chopped
½ cup onion, chopped
2 cloves garlic
2 - 15 ounce cans black beans, drained and rinsed
¼ cup water
1 teaspoon oregano
1 teaspoon cumin
1 bay leaf
1 teaspoon salt
¼ cup sherry
1 tablespoon red wine vinegar

Place the oil, bell pepper, onion, and garlic in a blender and process until smooth. Place the mixture in a large pot with the black beans and the remaining ingredients. Simmer for 1 hour, adding a little more water if necessary.

Total carbs 150g
About 22g carbs per ½ cup serving

Rice Bowl Guacamole

2 ripe avocados
1 jalapeño pepper, seeded and chopped
½ cup onion, finely chopped
2 tablespoons fresh cilantro or parsley, finely chopped
1 tablespoon lime juice
½ teaspoon salt

Using a fork, mash the avocados in a small bowl. Add the remaining ingredients, cover tightly with plastic wrap, and refrigerate, until ready to serve.

Total carbs 40g

Rice Bowl Lime Rice

½ onion, finely chopped
1 jalapeño pepper, seeded and minced
2 cloves garlic, minced
¼ cup lime juice
1 tablespoon parsley, chopped

2 cups chicken broth
1 cup water
1 teaspoon salt
1 tablespoon butter
1½ cups rice

Add all ingredients to a medium sauce pan. Bring to a boil over medium-high heat and then reduce to low heat. Cook until the rice is done, about 18-20 minutes.

Total carbs 240g

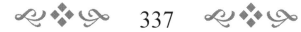

Ranch Pasta Salad

12 ounces uncooked GF noodles
10 slices of bacon

1 cup ranch dressing
¼ teaspoon garlic powder
½ teaspoon garlic pepper
½ teaspoon cayenne pepper
2 tomatoes, chopped
½ cup sliced black olives
1 cup shredded cheddar cheese

Cook the noodles according to the package directions. Drain, rinse, and cool. In a large skillet, cook the bacon. Once cooked, drain on a paper towel and crumble. Mix the remaining ingredients in a medium bowl. Add the noodles and bacon and mix well. Chill 1 hour before serving.

Total carbs 288g

Strawberry Spinach Salad

Dressing:
¼ cup sugar
¼ cup red wine vinegar
1 teaspoon prepared mustard
¼ teaspoon salt
¼ cup olive oil
1 teaspoon poppy seeds

Nuts:
½ cup broken pecan pieces
¼ teaspoon cinnamon

Salad:
6-8 cups baby spinach and lettuce mixed
½ cup red onion, chopped
3 cups strawberries, cut into large pieces,
      or 1 can drained mandarin oranges

Mix all dressing ingredients in a tightly sealing container and shake well. In a small bowl, toss the pecans with the cinnamon and toast at 350° for 5-8 minutes. Allow to cool. Place the spinach and lettuce in a large bowl. Top with the onions, strawberries, and toasted pecans. Drizzle the dressing over the top.

Carbs - About 15g carbs per 1 cup serving

Sweet Butternut Squash

1 large butternut squash

2 tablespoons butter
3 tablespoons milk
3 tablespoons maple syrup
½ teaspoon rum flavoring
¼ teaspoon cinnamon
¼ teaspoon nutmeg
1 teaspoon salt
½ teaspoon pepper

Poke the squash well with a knife. Cook squash in the microwave until soft, 18-20 minutes. Scoop the cooked squash into a large bowl and mash. Add remaining ingredients and mix well.

To avoid burnt fingers, you can cook the squash ahead of time and scoop it out once it's cooled. Then add the remaining ingredients and reheat in the microwave before serving.

Total carbs 150g

Sweet Potato Fries

¼ teaspoon cumin
1 clove garlic, crushed
3 tablespoons olive oil
½ teaspoon salt
2 large sweet potatoes, peeled and cut into wedges

Preheat the oven to 425°. Line a cookie sheet with foil and grease. Place cumin, garlic, oil, and salt in a large bowl. Add the sweet potatoes and toss to coat. Place the sweet potatoes on the cookie sheet. Bake for 35-40 minutes or until done.

Total carbs 200g

Thai Rice

2 cups water
1 cup jasmine rice
¼ cup green onions, chopped
1 teaspoon red curry paste
¼ teaspoon cayenne pepper
1 tablespoon cilantro
1 tablespoon butter
1 teaspoon fresh ginger, grated
¾ teaspoon turmeric
1 tablespoon lime juice

Roasted peanuts and red pepper flakes - for garnish

In a large sauce pan, combine all ingredients except peanuts and red pepper flakes. Bring to a boil, then lower the heat and simmer for 18-20 minutes or until the rice in done. Garnish with peanuts and red pepper flakes if desired.

Total carbs 160g

Turkish Tomato Sauce

(This goes well with Bursa Kabobs. Or add some shredded chicken and serve over noodles)

2 tablespoons olive oil
½ cup onion, chopped
2 cloves garlic, minced

1 - 28 ounce can crushed tomatoes
1 bay leaf
2 tablespoons fresh parsley, chopped
1 tablespoon fresh oregano, chopped
½ teaspoon sugar
½ teaspoon salt
½ teaspoon allspice
¼ teaspoon black pepper

Sauté the onions and garlic in the olive oil in a large sauce pan. Add the remaining ingredients and allow to simmer for 30 minutes.

Total carbs 60g
About 8g carbs per ½ cup

Notes:

Notes:

Snacks

Artichoke Dip

¾ cup mayonnaise
1¼ cups parmesan cheese
8 ounces cream cheese, softened
4 medium green onions
1 - 14 ounce can artichokes, cut up
1 - 10 ounce package frozen spinach, thawed and squeezed dry
2 cloves garlic, minced

GF crackers or tortilla chips

Preheat the oven to 400° and grease a 2.5 quart casserole dish. In a large bowl, mix all ingredients. Scoop the mixture into the prepared pan, and bake for 25-30 minutes. Serve with crackers or tortilla chips for dipping.

Total carbs 20g

Blueberry Cereal Bars

Crust:
1½ cups flour
1 cup GF oats
½ cup brown sugar
½ cup butter, melted
1 teaspoon xanthan gum

Filling:
1½ cups frozen blueberries – thawed
½ cup raisins

⅓ cup honey
1 tablespoon flour
½ teaspoon cinnamon
¼ teaspoon cloves

Quick Filling Option:
1 cup jam of any type

Optional:
¼ cup pecans, chopped

Preheat the oven to 350° and grease a 9x9 pan. In a small bowl, combine all ingredients for the crust. Pat half of the mixture into the bottom of the pan and set the other half aside.

Place all ingredients for the filling in a blender and puree until the mixture is smooth. Pour the mixture into a medium sauce pan and cook over medium-high heat for 1–2 minutes or until thick.

Pour the filling over the crust (or spread with jam for the quick option). Sprinkle the top with the reserved oat mixture and the pecans. Bake for 30-35 minutes or until lightly browned. Cool on a wire rack before cutting into rectangles. Store in the refrigerator or freezer.

Total carbs with home-made filling 530g
About 33g carbs per ¹⁄₁₆ piece

Deviled Eggs

6 hard-boiled eggs
3 tablespoons mayonnaise or ranch dressing
1 teaspoon prepared mustard
1 tablespoon pickle relish
⅛ teaspoon salt
¼ teaspoon pepper

Cut the eggs in half, lengthwise and scoop out the yolk into a medium bowl. Mash the yolks with a fork, then mix in the rest of the ingredients. Fill the egg whites with the yolk mixture. Cover and refrigerate until ready to serve.

For fun, try adding:

- 1 teaspoon chives and ½ teaspoon capers *or*
- ½ cup shredded cheese and 2 tablespoons chopped fresh parsley *or*
- Use 1 teaspoon horseradish instead of the prepared mustard *or*
- Be creative and make up your own!

No carbs!

Fresh Salsa

3 cups tomatoes, chopped
½ cup green onions, chopped
½ cup green bell peppers, chopped
3 tablespoons lime juice
2 tablespoons fresh parsley, chopped
3 cloves of garlic, finely chopped
1 tablespoon jalapeño chilies, finely chopped
½ teaspoon salt

Mix all the ingredients and refrigerate.

For fun: Try adding black beans or hot sauce

Total carbs 35g

Grandma Toni's Cheese Ball

1 pound medium cheddar cheese, finely grated
8 ounces cream cheese
2 teaspoons onion powder

Chopped nuts or parsley

Have cheeses at room temperature. Mix all ingredients in a large bowl. Use a pastry cutter to mix until well incorporated. Form the cheese into one large or two smaller balls. Roll in chopped nuts or parsley, or both. Keep in the refrigerator, but bring to room temperature before serving. These can be frozen.

For fun: Add some different cheeses to the mix. Just make sure they're gluten free.

No Carbs!

Granola Bars

3 cups GF oats
1 cup nuts of your choice, coarsely chopped
1 cup raisins or other dried fruit
1½ teaspoons cinnamon
1 - 14 ounce can sweetened condensed milk
½ cup butter, melted

Optional additions: coconut, sesame seeds, sunflower seeds, anything else that sounds good.

Preheat the oven to 320°. Line a rimmed cookie sheet with foil and grease. Mix all the granola ingredients in a large bowl and press evenly onto the cookie sheet. Bake for about 45 minutes, watching carefully so the edges don't burn. Cool a little and then flip the bars onto a cutting board. Cut into bars. Once they've cooled completely, place them in snack bags and store in the fridge or freezer. Makes about 28 bars.

Total carbs 700g -without adding additional ingredients
About 25g carbs per bar

Guacamole

2 ripe avocados, peeled and seed removed
½ teaspoon ground cumin
¼-½ cup tomatoes, seeded and chopped
¼ cup onion, finely chopped
1 clove garlic, minced
1 jalapeño chili, seeded and minced
2 tablespoons fresh parsley, chopped
2 tablespoons lime juice
1 teaspoon salt
½ teaspoon black pepper
¼ teaspoon ground red pepper

Using a fork, mash the avocados in a medium bowl. Add the remaining ingredients and mix well. Cover and refrigerate until ready to serve.

Total carbs 40g

No-Bake Apple Bars

4 cups GF rice or cinnamon cereal
⅔ cup dried apples, chopped
½ cup sliced almonds
½ cup dried cranberries

1 tablespoon butter
½ cup light corn syrup
¼ cup brown sugar

Line a 9x9 pan with foil and spray with cooking oil. In a large bowl, mix the cereal, apples, almonds, and cranberries. In a saucepan heat the butter, corn syrup, and brown sugar. Cook for 2 minutes, stirring constantly until slightly thickened.

Pour over the cereal mixture and stir well. Press into the prepared pan and refrigerate for 1 hour. Once they've cooled completely, cut into bars. Place them in snack bags and store in the fridge or freezer. Makes about 16 bars.

Total carbs 335g
About 21g carbs per bar

Plum Applesauce

5 large apples (about 2 pounds)
5 plums (about 1½ pounds)
¼ cup apple juice
¼ cup sugar
1 cinnamon stick
4 tablespoons butter

Cut up the fruit, leaving the skins on. Place in a crock pot with the remaining ingredients and cook on high for 1½-2 hours. Remove the cinnamon stick. Mash the fruit with a potato masher. Serve warm or cold.

Total carbs 180g

Sugar Coated Pecans

1 egg white
1 tablespoon water

1 pound pecan halves
1 cup white sugar
¼ teaspoon salt
½ teaspoon cinnamon

Preheat the oven to 250°. Line a cookie sheet with foil and grease the foil. In a large bowl mix the egg white and water until frothy. Add the remaining ingredients and mix well. Spread the nuts on the cookie sheet. Bake for 1 hour, stirring every 15 minutes.

Carbs 200g
About 2g carbs per pecan

Texas Caviar

1 - 15 ounce can black beans, drained and rinsed
1 - 15 ounce can petite diced, tomatoes, drained
2 medium jalapeño chilies, seeded and minced
1 small onion, minced
½ red bell pepper, diced
¼ cup fresh cilantro or parsley
6 tablespoons red wine vinegar
¼ cup olive oil
1½ teaspoons cumin
½ teaspoon salt
½ teaspoon pepper
1 teaspoon garlic powder
1 teaspoon oregano

GF tortilla chips

Mix all the ingredients in a medium bowl. Cover and refrigerate for 2 hours. Serve with tortilla chips.

Total carbs 105g

Notes:

Menus

All the main dish recipes have been divided into six recipes per week with a variety of flavors. This can be used to simplify shopping for the week and also provides the chance to try different recipes.

There are twenty three weeks total, so you can go almost half a year without making the same meal twice.

Week 1

Rice, Beans, and Brats
Fajitas
Creamy Chicken and Broccoli Soup
Blackberry Balsamic Chicken
Swiss Steak
Chicken Pizza

Week 2

Crock Pot Orange Chicken
Baked Beef Stew
Chicken with Caramelized Onions
Basic Meatloaf
Pizza
Chicken Noodle Soup

Week 3

Ham and Cheese Melts
Thai Chicken with Peanut Sauce
Maple Pork Chops
Cranberry Chicken
Cincinnati Chili
Moroccan Tomato Soup

Week 5

Zesty Grilled Chicken
Tom Ka Chicken
Chicken Tortilla Soup
Moroccan Beef or Lamb Patties
Polynesian Meatballs
Coconut Chicken

Week 7

Quick Italian chicken
Szechwan Stir-Fry
Opa's Fried Chicken
Beef Stroganoff
Sausage and Bean Skillet
Pepperoni Soup

Week 4

Super Easy Crock Pot Roast/or Pot Roast
Shepherd's Pie
Chicken with Creamy Mustard Sauce
Oven BBQ ribs
Sweet and Spicy Mexican Chicken
Corn Chowder

Week 6

Ham with Pear Topping
Potato Soup with Bacon
Tacos
Sauerbraten Pot Roast
Lemon Basil Chicken
Chimichangas

Week 8

Korean Marinated Beef
Taco Soup
Festive Taco Lasagna
BBQ Pork Sandwiches
Chicken and Mushroom Fettuccine
Chicken Tikka

Week 9

Curried Apricot chicken
Spaghetti
Chili Soup
Overnight Spiced Chicken
Home-style Beef and Noodles
Lemon Roasted Chicken

Week 11

Saucy Pesto Chicken
Chicken Basil Stir Fry
Salisbury Steak
Pork and Apple Skewers
Spinach-Stuffed Shells
Orange-Glazed Chicken Tenders

Week 13

Brown Rice Chicken Casserole
Glazed Ginger Chicken
Black Bean Pie
Italian Sausage Pasta
Cheeseburger Salad
Italian Spiced Meatballs

Week 10

Bolognese Pasta Sauce
Refried Bean Soup
Super Easy Crock Pot Ham
Simple Parmesan Chicken
Ham and Cheese Meat Roll
Bursa Kabobs

Week 12

Ham and Bean Soup
Vegetable Lasagna
Tex-Mex Chili
Chicken with Wine Sauce
Quiche or Crustless Spinach Quiche
Italian Lost Toast

Week 14

Chicken in a Pot
Andy's Enchilada Hot Dish
Potato Toppers
Macaroni and Cheese
Sweet Potato and Black Bean Soup
Macaroni, Ham and Cheese Salad

Week 15

Ranch Chicken Skewers
Mulligatawny Stew
Enchilada Chicken Pizza
Red Chicken
Amish Breakfast Casserole/
        Breakfast for Dinner
Inner Mongolian Stir Fry

Week 16

Apricot Pork chops
Spicy Chicken "Wings"
Thai Leek Stir Fry
Southwest Meatloaf
Mozzarella Stuffed Chicken Rolls
Cannellini Bean and Sausage Stew

Week 17

Artichoke Chicken Bake
Potato Sausage Skillet
Take-Out Lemon Chicken
Cheese Fondue
Potato Swiss Chowder
Maple Glazed Chicken

Week 18

Opa's Fried Chicken Nuggets
Pizza in a Bowl
Fiesta Chicken Burritos
Tangy BBQ Pork
Ham and Split Pea Soup
Beef Tenderloin with Balsamic Sauce

Week 19

Basic Beef Stew
Manicotti
African Chicken Soup
Curried BBQ Chicken
Potato Lasagna
Fiery Chicken Stir Fry

Week 20

Mexican Rice Bowls
Southwest Pork
Nacho Cheese Soup
Peanutty Indonesian Ch. Skewers
Pepper Steak
Volcano Meatballs

Week 21

Black Bean Soup
Sloppy Joes
Sweet and Sour Pork/Meatballs
Creamy Thai Baked Chicken
Indian Chicken Patties
Potato Bacon Casserole

Week 23

Quick Nachos
Ham Alfredo
Deep Dish Pizza
Kaia's Spiced Chicken
Mexican Chicken Skillet
Mediterranean Beef Pitas

Week 22

Zucchini Boats
White Chicken Chili
Molasses Baked Chicken
Cornflake Chicken
French Dip Sandwiches
London Broil with Onions

Index

Bars

Beef

Breakfast

 368

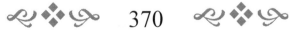

370

Soups

Yeast Breads

Notes:

Notes:

Notes:

Notes:

Notes:

Notes:

Notes:

A special thanks to those who helped
put this book together:

Jane Brohmer
Suzanne Marty
Liesel Ose

About the Author:

Heidi L. Likins has been an RN for over twenty years, a celiac for more than ten and celiac educator for over eight, teaching newly diagnosed celiacs how to navigate a gluten free diet. She is Mom to three hungry teens, and "Mom" to a crowd of their even hungrier friends. Her current position is that of education coordinator at a health care facility in beautiful Colorado.

Heidi Likins RN, BSN, CRRN

Made in the USA
Columbia, SC
14 November 2017